Praise for Power to Thrive

"Rich Cavaness believes in choices. In "Power to Thrive," he provides numerous ways for you to choose to be the person God desires you to be. You will be challenged: four questions to answer to escape mediocrity. You will be educated: learn the real definition of FEAR. You will be assured: you were created with everything you need for greatness! You will be inspired: God's "personal" words for you. As you can see, Rich will touch your head and your heart and your soul."

Bryan Flanagan, Flanagan Training Group

"Power to Thrive will get you thinking differently, bigger, and more focused on your true potential! Your real PURPOSE is right around the corner and starts on page 1 of this book. Very educational, inspiring and motivating. Proud of you, Rich! You've written a WINNER, my friend."

Cody Askins, #1 insurance sales trainer in the world and founder of 8% Nation

In his book, "Power to Thrive," author Rich Cavaness skillfully addresses the lies that so easily keep us from being all that God created us to be! Using an abundance of scripture and thought- provoking questions, Rich takes you on a journey of self-discovery and growth!

Elizabeth B. Mahusay, Author of the book, "Transform My Thinking God" Speaker, Sales & Leadership Coach

"Power to Thrive, is a must read for anyone who desires to take hopes and dreams *to the next level. The solid biblical approach plus the practical steps offer in every chapter create a clear and doable roadmap towards a thriving life."*

Ruber J. Leal, Founder and Speaker of ForeverONE© Ministries.

"*Power to Thrive is a powerful, thought provoking, spiritual think tank. I love how Rich combines biblical principles, scientific research, and personal experience to craft a success plan for personal well-being and life development. The end of chapter questions are thought provoking and inspiring. Whether you're looking to improve your walk with Christ, create a better life for yourself and your family, or discover your special gifts and talents, this book will not only inspire you but give you the tools to be your best self, the way God intended.*"

Lisa Hammett, Success Coach - Personal, Professional, Philanthropic

"*This book brings a great blend of relevant stories from others, Scripture, and thought- provoking questions, all topped off with Rich's own wisdom and experience. Power to Thrive will help you understand that you are one of God's magnificent creations and your worth is in Him and will take you from a mindset of negativity and being set in your comfort zone, to that of striving and thriving. He will help you break the status of mediocrity to a new place of excellence. Power to Thrive could easily be put in a category of "Must read for a balanced life".*"

Steve Reed, Best Selling Author, Speaker, and Ziglar Choose to Win Coach

"*Too many people struggle in life and wander through their lives, never knowing what they were put on this planet to accomplish. In Rich's new book, "Power to Thrive," you will discover not only your identity but also how to function at your highest level in life. This is a must- read for high achievers.*"

Pastor Kendall Bridges of Freedom Church and Author of *Better Marriage Against All Odds, Never Settle for Good Enough* and *Better Day* - One Year Devotional

"Power to Thrive" is the blueprint for your journey as you unlock the power you have been given to thrive. Rich's life experience, handling of scripture, and methodical use of questions give you what you need to be both inspired and accountable while chasing your dreams."
Aaron Mitchell, Christian author of the
book, *The New Testament Challenge*

"Identity, Purpose, Success, Peace, Joy, Fulfillment. The hope to leave a growing legacy while enjoying a fulfilling retirement. To be a great leader, influencer, spouse, or parent. These are great dreams, aspirations but what Power to Thrive does is magnify the core. We have been given breath by God. We have nothing without Him, but in Him, we have everything. Rich peels back the "onion layers" of ideas, uncovering the real source of freedom. This book will ignite your life!
Eric Coburn, Senior Pastor of Calvary Chapel Church

"If you've ever been around Rich Cavaness, you'll see his passion pouring out in this book. He covers every aspect of goals and living a life with purpose. You can tell that Rich has poured his heart out in this book, and if you take time to go through the exercises included in the book, you'll see the progress you can make to a life that is thriving. Great job, Rich!
Lyle Leads, CEO of DFW Top Business and
Branding and Digital Marketing Strategist

"Power to Thrive is a phenomenal, super informative, super detailed, super-effective book with actionable steps on how to apply the content that you read. Power to Thrive is going to do great good for any person who decides to read and apply the principles Rich teaches."
Ryan D. Lee, Owner and Founder of
Cashflow Tactics and Altitude Life

"*Power to Thrive is a must- read for every Christian who wants to truly understand the wonderful gifts our Creator and Redeemer has given each of us to thrive in this world.*

This book is great for self- study and reflection, and it would also be a wonderful small group study. Get it, read it, study it, and put the power to thrive in your life!"

Tom Bronson, founder of Mastery Partners
and author of Maximize Business Value

"*The Power to Thrive will give you rock solid advice in helping you put together a plan of action in helping you discover God's plan for our life. This is a must read, practical, applicable and refreshing, I loved it. I want to order 10 books already, this is a New York Times bestseller for sure!.*

Rob Bliss, CEO/Chief Sales Guy, SmartOffice USA

"*I love your book! It is a comprehensive work that will help the reader reframe and re-write their internal belief system. I loved the insights on what you can control and what we worry about. How much of our lives is dependent on what we think about ourselves and the impact knowing God desires for each of us to reach our full potential, thriving in every way.*"

Patrick Dougher, CEO Doer Success
Systems, Speaker, Author and Coach

"*Power to Thrive is not your typical self-help book. It is packed with scientific research and Biblical wisdom that will transform your life. Rich masterfully weaves anecdote and expertise to clearly show anyone how to Rise above mediocrity, Unlock your God-given power, and Elevate your everyday living.*"

David Jamieson, Senior Pastor of Church
in the Valley, Langley, BC, Canada

"Some Christians struggle with the idea of positive mindset training and personal growth beyond the Bible itself. Then there are non-Christians who struggle with seeing the value and truth in the Bible. Rich Cavaness' book "Power to Thrive" bridges the gap with clear principles, undeniable truth and practical steps to live forward."

Bill McConnell, CEO & Founder of
Journey Shift and Your Clarity Blueprint

"In his book, "Power to Thrive," Rich joins the ranks of outstanding authors who have had the courage, and shown the authenticity, to face their adversities head on, and to find solutions and answers in some very difficult places. Pulling from his own journey of struggles and solutions with a lens towards THRIVING, Rich has gifted all of us with 17 incredible chapters that kept me riveted on every page. I especially loved the "RISING ABOVE MEDICRITY" Manifesto, which helps any of us to transform our life and business with a belief in God and His power to flow in you and through you! From mindset to limiting beliefs, to learning the right kind of self-talk and financial freedom, Rich's passion to help others is evident, and you will enjoy his energy, his passion, and his practical approach to some common challenges."

Abe Brown, MBA, CMCP, Founder,
Flourishing Life Coaching

"Power to Thrive will change your life. The power of God combined with the power of a positive mindset and the organized, no-excuses plan to success presented in this book will transform you from average to everything God wants you to be. This book is a must-read for anyone who wants to thrive with God."

Stewart Pepper, Senior Pastor, Pittsburgh
Seventh-day Adventist Church

"I really loved the book Power To Thrive! All of us are over loaded with life. We are limited in how to spend our time. This book puts in perspective how we can focus on things that are most important. That focus is on spiritual matters as it is the source of all that is good and all our blessings both spiritual and material. That source is the Lord Jesus Christ. Without this vision, people perish!"

Dr. Reynardo Adorable, DC, FIACA

"In Power to Thrive, Rich shows a path and the fundamentals for how to gain purpose and reach the personal best and the greatness that God has planned for me. Rich reveals Biblical truths about the magnificent possibilities that I can reach by making the best choices. No more living in fear, no more mediocrity, no more regret. Time to THRIVE!"

Dean Hansen, Farmers Insurance Agency Owner

"When the student is ready, the teacher appears" has never been more so than the lessons to be learned in this incredible book. I personally needed the chapter on forgiveness and it has freed my soul! Do your-self a favor and promise to not only read it once, but refer back to it constantly as a guide to being the person God intended for you to be."

Petey Parker, Owner at Your Hiring Partners
and speaker and consultant

POWER TO THRIVE

ELEVATE YOUR EVERYDAY LIVING BY UNLOCKING YOUR GOD-GIVEN POWER SO YOU CAN RISE ABOVE MEDIOCRITY

RICHARD J. CAVANESS

Edited by Kim Bentson & Apryl Hall
Printed by Ingram Spark & KDP by Amazon
Front and Back Cover Design by Jetlaunch
Interior Art and Design by Jetlaunch
Author Photo by Fred Mahusay Photography

Printed in United States of America
Cavaness Enterprises, LLC
Dallas, TX 75287
www.PowerToThrive.net
www.RichCavaness.com
www.TheGratitudeEffect.net

ISBN:
Paperback 978-1-64184-626-4
Ebook 978-1-64184-627-1

"For God has not given us a spirit of fear, but of power and of love and of a sound mind."
2 Timothy 1:7 (NKJV)

Contents

Part One

Knowing Your Identity is the KEY to Thriving in Life

Part Two

Your Outer World is a Direct Reflection of Your Inner World

Part Three

Physical and Mental Health Will Lead to Emotional Well-Being

The Thriver's Manifesto

1. The greatest gift God gave you is the **power to choose.** Your choices determine where you end up in life, period!

2. When you accept 100% responsibility for your life—the good, the bad, successes, and defeats—you open the door to living the abundant life God has for you.

3. Your lot in life is not **set or determined;** you are a potential genius. You can grow, change and solve problems no matter who you are or where you were born.

4. You were created in the image of God with great, untapped reserves of potential within you and a purpose. Your mission in life is to discover and **release** them.

5. Acknowledge that Jesus Christ is your Lord and Savior and through the power He gives us through the Holy Spirit helps us overcome the challenges of this world in every way imaginable.

6. It doesn't matter where you are from or what you have done; all that matters is where you are **going and what you are doing today**.

7. There are no limits on what you can achieve with your life except the limits you accept in **your mind**. If you change your **thinking,** you can change your life!

8. Everything you want in life is attainable if you press through your **fears**!

9. Your success will be primarily determined by your ability to **concentrate and focus** single-mindedly on one thing at a time.

10. If there is anything you want in life, find out how others have achieved it and do the same things.

11. It's not what you say, or wish, or hope, or intend; it is what you **DO** that counts. Action is the fuel for your dreams!

12. Everyone has an emotional bank account. You either build it up by depositing life and positivity into it or **tear** it down by sowing negativity and limits into it.

13. Ultimately, if you don't plan your life, someone or something will do it for you. Live Your Life by Design! You are the master architect of your life.

Foreword

I believe you were hardwired to **THRIVE.** God placed within you the tools and abilities to take dominion in life and prosper. The question then becomes, "Why do so many people merely survive versus thrive?" Somewhere along the way, we lose our confidence. We lose our way. Instead of finding our voice and moving into vocations, we stumble into a job, an occupation. We lose our confidence and begin believing a great lie that this was all we were intended to do, merely survive.

If you are looking for more, then you are looking in the right place. Rich uses the word equip in this book. This book is a new way of life. It activates a new drive in you to prosper, move toward your abundance, and move from surviving to thriving. It helps you find and discover your God-given talents and get in alignment with your true potential. It's about forming new thoughts, reconnecting to your core, and remembering where your true talents come from, finding those talents, and distributing those talents to the world.

You were not given a spirit of fear. If you were to look up the definition of fear in the dictionary, it says, "a negative emotion created by a belief that someone or something is going to harm us in the future." I believe fear is the work of the devil. He convinces you to contract versus expanding. This book is about expansion. This book is about courage. This book is about using your talents to **THRIVE** in a world where so many appear alive but are dead.

I've worked with Rich Cavaness on multiple occasions as a coach and mentor. He is humble, hungry, and teachable and is ready to bring this book and his message to the world.

Go deep in it. Meditate on it. Believe it. And use it to **THRIVE** in the world.

The word power is a "means or source for supplying energy." God is your power source, and this book is the road map.

Coach Micheal Burt
17X author
Founder, The Greatness Factory

Introduction

"I guess it comes down to a simple choice, really.
Get busy living or get busy dying."
Andy Dufresne, from *Shawshank*
Redemption, played by Tim Robbins

"For God has not given us a spirit of fear, but of
power and of love and of a sound mind."
2 Timothy 1:7 (NKJV)

Congratulations! You are about to embark on a journey of adventure and discovery that will enable you to accomplish *more* in the next several months than many people accomplish in ten years or even in their lifetime.

Power to Thrive has been building since I began my research, study, and practice of the principles and concepts inside over 30 years ago. As a young, budding entrepreneur, I learned the things written in this book from hundreds of others that went before me. The success I enjoy today results from learning from great teachers and following the most extraordinary success book of all time: The Bible, which is God's Holy Word. The concepts and subjects that you will learn about while reading this book have taken many tens of thousands of men and women from living in mediocrity to living their God-given purpose and using their gifts, talents, and abilities.

I am a self-taught man who started my adult life out getting a degree in Ski Instruction/Coaching from a small school in Wenatchee, WA. Being in the skiing industry as a professional skier and ski school director was the stepping stone for me in speaking, coaching, sales, and writing books and content. Since then, I have read hundreds upon hundreds of books, attended scores of seminars, purchased coaching programs, hired my personal coaches, listened to online training and development programs, became a certified master coach practitioner, and a certified instructor with the Napoleon Hill Foundation. Since the early 1990s, I have uncovered the science of success between the Bible, the Positive Psychology movement, and personal development strategies. These fundamental principles help individuals live the life of their dreams. I know from personal experience they work because I have applied these principles to my own life.

I know you are 100% able to achieve the same results. I know for a fact that you can attain no-limits living and out of this universe success because you will learn the principles and concepts that have helped tens of thousands of others achieve their dreams. You were created and designed for greatness and given unique gifts. There is a reason for you being alive, and only God can give you the power to achieve it. When you combine time-tested principles with God's given plan for you, that is a formula that **GUARANTEES success!**

The ideas you are going to learn are tested and proven. When you read and then apply the principles, you will have a blueprint to begin accomplishing the most meaningful things in your life. All you have to do is decide what it is you want for your life, believe that you deserve it and that God wants you to have it, and then put the concepts of *Power to Thrive* to work in your life.

Professional sports have a season of training and exhibition games before they start their official season because they are working on the fundamentals and basics of their sport. They are getting their muscle memory back on track by repeating over and over again the right moves, techniques, and patterns. It's the same with personal development fundamentals and *Power to Thrive*. The fundamentals described within this book are the same for people in every profession and all walks of life. If you learn them and then apply them with focus and discipline every day, these fundamentals will transform your life beyond what you could think or imagine.

Power to Thrive specifically addresses the **seven main obstacles to success** that God created you to have:

- Not knowing your WHY or WHERE you are going in your life

- Fear of leaving your comfort zone

- Excess stress and personal health issues

- Limiting beliefs holding you back

- A negative mindset that is not conducive to living an abundant life

- Having a lack of emotional control

- Not tapping into God's power and plan for your life

All of life is a matter of habit. Successful, high-achieving people are simply those with habits that led to success and where they wanted to go. You can learn the habits you need to escape mediocrity, unlock your God-given power, and elevate your everyday living. Upon doing so, your wonderful future of health, wealth, and happiness is assured. After all, you are the captain of your ship; you are the designer of your destiny.

Please remember that success takes time. Your transformation will not happen overnight. Success requires that you have effort, energy, discipline, perseverance, and patience with yourself. Take *Power to Thrive* seriously, apply the principles, and do the end-of-chapter discussion questions in this book. You will begin to rise above mediocrity and reach your God-given potential. You will see your dreams more clearly and develop a pathway making them come to life. You will see a new person begin to emerge when you look at yourself in the mirror and begin to peel away the layers of untruth, past lies, and limiting beliefs.

Positive change is possible, and it will happen for you with challenges arising along the way. Love yourself enough not to give up. Love yourself enough to be patient and kind to yourself. Love yourself enough to believe that God has created you for a unique purpose and that you have Divine DNA flowing through your blood. Remember, you can do all things through Christ who gives you strength. Today is Day One of escaping the prison of mediocrity, unlocking your God-given power, and elevating your everyday living.

How to Apply the Power to Thrive Principles

Power to Thrive is designed to be used in conjunction with online coaching programs and live weekend events, but it isn't necessary. *Power to Thrive* is going to be a very personal book for you. I encourage you to make notes in it, apply the principles discussed, and write down notes about what is important to you. You will find yourself returning to your *Power to Thrive* book repeatedly in the weeks and months following the reading of the material.

At the end of each chapter is a **Thinking About** section with questions. I encourage you to take time to answer these questions before moving to the next chapter. This section will allow you to consider what you just read and how it applies to you personally and provides a place to write down your thoughts and reflect upon them.

The book enables you to decide precisely what you want in every area of your life and then help you achieve it. Of course, you cannot change everything overnight, so the idea is to take steady steps in each chapter covered.

A significant theme of *Power to Thrive* is that you can have anything you want, as long as you know what that is. *Clarity* is essential. People are stuck in mediocrity in life, not because they lack ability or opportunity, but because they lack clarity about their purpose, goals, values, mission, God-ordained gifts, beliefs, attitudes, and habits.

Power to Thrive will become a personal action plan for becoming who you want and accomplishing what you want. It's going to take hard, systematic work and self-discipline. Investing in yourself every day is the real habit of success. Continuous action towards your goals must take place as long as you have breath.

The end game for you? You will have complete charge of your life and turn yourself into an unstoppable, divinely inspired, values-driven, courageous, positive, goal-oriented, self-confident, persistent, personal achievement machine!

Remember God's words in Philippians 4:13, "I can do **ALL** things through Christ who gives me strength."

PART ONE

Knowing Your Identity is the KEY to Thriving in Life

*"You weren't an accident. You weren't mass pro-
duced. You aren't an assembly-line product. You were
deliberately planned, specifically gifted, and lovingly posi-
tioned on the earth by the Master Craftsman."*
Max Lucado, best-selling Christian author

"And the Lord God formed man of the dust of the
ground, and breathed into his nostrils the breath
of life; and man became a living being."
Genesis 2:7 (NKJV)

1

Don't Look Now. You've Been Hacked!

"The major strategy of Satan is to distort the character of God and the truth of who we are. He can't change God and he can't do anything to change our identity and position in Christ. If, however, he can get us to believe a lie, we will live as though our identity in Christ isn't true."
Neil T. Anderson, author and ministry leader

"You will know the truth, and the truth will make you free."
John 8:32 (ERV)

What do Yahoo, Marriott, eBay, Equifax, Macy's, Target, Capital One, Home Depot, Adidas, Planet Hollywood, Kay Jewelers, Saks Fifth Avenue, Panera Bread, and Cheddars all have in common?

The answer is that these well-established brands and businesses have experienced a significant security breach in their database systems. They got hacked, and millions of customers got their information and identity stolen. The criminals that hacked these systems make money off your name by going shopping, obtaining loans, and filling out phony tax returns on your behalf.

Data breaches exposed 4.1 billion records in the first six months of 2019 (Forbes).

As of 2019, cyber-attacks are among the top five risks to global stability (World Economic Forum).

These hacks are dangerous, very costly, and often the damage is irreversible. Identity theft is a massive hassle, taking months and years for victims to recover.

As bad as commercial identity theft is today, did you know there is another identity theft happening today that is much worse?

This identity theft targets all people from all walks of life, and its origination comes from none other than the master of all lies, the greatest deceiver ever to live. Yes, it's the devil himself.

In Genesis, we find in the first pages of the Bible how everything began and came into being. And in verse 26, the details are given about our identity and what God's desire was for us as He put the plans together to create humanity, "Then God said, "Let Us make man in Our image, according to Our likeness... So God created man in His own image; in the image of God He created him; male and female He created them," Genesis 1:26-27 (NKJV).

In chapter two, more details are explicitly given on how the very hands of God Himself created both man and woman. Not from an unintentional freak blast from the universe, not from a tadpole or pond scum, not even from apes or caveman, but from God's very own hand with His mind and with His intention and purpose: "And the Lord God formed man of the dust of the ground, and breathed into his nostrils the breath of life; and man became a living being," Genesis 2:7 (NKJV).

Later in chapter two, God did not want the man to be alone, so he created a companion, a helpmate for him, out of his rib. Notice what it says in Verse 23: "And Adam said, 'This is now bone of my bones, and flesh of my flesh; she shall be called Woman, because she was taken out of Man.'" Genesis 2:23 (KJ21).

But then came the hacking and identity theft of mankind. Both man and woman got their identities hacked and stolen by the wise serpent called the Devil himself.

The entire premise behind the temptation and fall of Adam and Eve in the very beginning had to do with identity. In Genesis 3:4-5, the hacking takes place, "Then the serpent said to the woman, 'You will not surely die. For God knows that in the day you eat of it your eyes will be opened, and you will be like God, knowing good and evil.'" (NKJV)

The Devil's master lies revolved around the theme of identity. He convinced Eve she needed to create her OWN identity outside of what God created her to be because WHO and WHAT God created her to be is NOT enough! The devil was essentially telling Eve, "you are not good enough in the identity the Creator of the Universe has given to you, so we need to create our own identity apart from God."

My question for you today is this: How has your identity been hacked? How do you find your own identity today? Many of us live out our identity much differently than God's intended purpose and plan for us. See if any of these sound or feel familiar to you:

- **Athletics and sports.** Often people live out their past glory days and become very performance or results-based as part of their identity.

- **Material Items.** People can find their identity through their possessions, houses, cars, technology, jewelry, investments, and businesses.

5

- **Career and achievements.** Many people identify themselves with their achievements, degrees, certifications, jobs, and professional titles.

- **Intellect or education.** Some people feel their entire identity is relative to how smart or how stupid they think they are.

- **Family and people.** Many people's identity is tied to their relationships, especially parents who try to live vicariously through their children.

Another way we live by a false identity is by internalizing what others say about us. Living this way can have deep-seated impacts, especially if you grew up in a home or environment where someone told you that you weren't enough, you were a loser, or that you would never become successful or prosperous.

One of the most significant areas of false identity comes from the things we do to ourselves. When we make mistakes or experience defeat in our lives, we often define ourselves by these past events. We spend huge amounts of our time living in the rear-view mirror of life instead of looking out the front window at what's ahead for us.

Then, to top it off, we often turn to drugs, alcohol, stealing, affairs, and lying. After all the collateral damage adds up, we label ourselves and begin to live out a false identity such as alcoholic, adulterer, liar, thief, and druggie. Yes, you may have done those things, you may be doing them right now, but those have nothing to do with your actual identity.

You are not what you do, and you are not what you become; you are not what others say about you. You are a creation of the almighty God of the Universe. Understanding this truth is critical for you as you read this book.

First and foremost, your identity is that you are made in the image and likeness of God, the Creator of the universe. And nothing you can do can add to that value because God created it in the first place.

Here is how God describes you in the Bible:

- Psalm 139:13-17: you are fearfully and wonderfully made

- Ephesians 2:10: you are God's workmanship, created to live out His purpose for you

- Romans 8:37: you are more than a conqueror through Him who loves you

- 2 Timothy 1:7 you were not made to live in fear, but to be powerful, loving, and have an abundance mindset

- Colossians 2:10: you are complete in Him who is the head over all rule and authority, including all angelic and earthly powers.

- John 1:12: you are the child of the Most-High God

- John 15:15: you are a friend of God, chose by Him

- 1 Corinthians 2:16: you have the mind of Christ Jesus your Lord

- Philippians 4:13: you can do all things through Jesus Christ who gives you strength

- Ephesians 1:7: you are redeemed and forgiven of all your sins and made clean by the blood of Jesus Christ

- Ephesians 2:4: you are loved greatly by God and chosen by Him

- Colossians 1:11: you are strengthened with all power according to His glorious might

- Philippians 4:19: you are supplied with all your needs according to God's love for you

Even though the devil may have hacked or stolen your identity, the God who made you and designed you for greatness has a different message about your identity and who you are. The devil will try to convince you that you're not good enough, unloved, inadequate, unworthy, damaged goods, and hopeless. Allow the truth of God's holy word to sink in: you are a child of God, divine creation of the Creator of the Universe, who He made for a purpose with definite intention.

It's time to embrace a different view of yourself through the lens of God. It's time for you to stop living in the false identity of who you think you are and start living the true identity God created you with for His glory and honor.

Chapter two explicitly gives more details how the very hands of God Himself created both man and woman.

Thinking About My Identity Being Hacked

How has your view about yourself impacted and guided your life?

How does your view of God as Creator change the way you look at life after reading this chapter?

How does being made in the image and likeness of God impress upon your mind the value and worth that you have?

How can fully understanding that you are nature's greatest miracle change how you view others and your relationships?

What impact does this statement have on your life: You are not what you do, you are not what you become, you are not what others say about you; you are a creation of the almighty God of the Universe.

2

The Four Questions You Have to Answer to Escape Mediocrity

"What I think the DNA material has done is that it
has shown, by the almost unbelievable complexity of
the arrangements which are needed to produce life, that
intelligence must have been involved in getting these
extraordinarily diverse elements to work together."
—Anthony Flew, English philosopher

"For You formed my inward parts; You covered me in my
mother's womb. I will praise You, for I am fearfully and
wonderfully made; Marvelous are Your works, and that my
soul knows very well. My frame was not hidden from You,
When I was made in secret, and skillfully wrought in the
lowest parts of the earth. Your eyes saw my substance, being

yet unformed. In Your book they all were written, the days fashioned for me, when as yet there were none of them."
Psalm 139:13-16 (NKJV)

From ages four to eleven, I was raised in Phoenix, Arizona. My great-grandparents lived in Lakeside, Arizona, a beautiful place in the White Mountains of the state. I used to spend lots of time during my summers off from school with my grandparents. I loved seeing the giant ponderosa pines around their house, going for hikes, and exploring the area. It was a magical and emotionally fulfilling experience for me that I looked forward to each summer.

I remember once my Grandpa and I went up into the mountains to do some fishing and camping over the weekend. It was nighttime, and it was dark. We had a small campfire, and we lay next to each other, looking up at the stars and the universe. I remember being in such awe. I was overwhelmed by the immensity and beauty of what we saw.

That night I saw shooting stars and a bright, luminous half-moon. My grandpa showed me the North Star, the Big and Little Dippers, and the planet Venus. As a young boy, I began to entertain the question of who could have done this? How did this all come about?

What happened to me that night, for sure, is that I tapped into my spiritual self. I knew that nature, the cosmos, all of creation were going to be a place of peace, serenity, and connection with my Creator for me. Anything in nature, even to this very day, makes me draw inward. I am grateful for all of creation and what nature provides for me each and every day.

Most major religions see everything around from the ground to the cosmos, created by a supreme being or power and Intelligent Design. The universe exists under perfect law, with order and obedience to law pointing to clear intelligent creation for a definite purpose and plan. Just the fact that the universe has order seems to indicate the presence of creative power and design by infinite intelligence.

Walter L. Bradley, Distinguished Professor of Engineering at Baylor University, explains this idea clearly in his published article, "Is There Scientific Evidence for the Existence of God? How the Recent Discoveries Support a Designed Universe." Bradley states science proves beyond a shadow of a doubt that not only is there infinite creative design, but it appears the design was intended specifically for human life to exist. Every process of nature has order with no evidence of chance. A key point of Bradley's is this, "The design requirements for our universe are like a chain of 1,000 links. If any link breaks, we do not have a less optimal universe for life -- we have a universe incapable of sustaining life!"

Think about gravity, temperature, oxygen, vegetation, distance from the sun to the earth, all the elements that make up our world, and how everything operates perfectly. They allow our life to be able to exist in perfect harmony on this planet we call earth.

Every person born into this world has to wrestle and come to their own conclusions with the **four basic questions of life,** which determine your identity, sense of worth, and meaning to your life. **The four questions are:**

- **Who am I?**
- **Why am I here?**
- **Where did I come from?**
- **What happens when I die?**

There are two basic philosophies, beliefs, religions, and faith that predominantly cover these four questions. Still, each one has an entirely different outcome and direction for your life. The belief systems I am referring to are Creation and Evolution.

The basic premise of each system is that Creationism or Intelligent Design believes that life and the universe were created by a supernatural being (an "intelligent designer"), an omnipotent, benevolent God. Evolution is the process by which different kinds of living organisms developed and diversified from earlier forms during the earth's history.

Now some of you might be asking yourselves, "Why do we even squabble over creation versus evolution? Does it matter what we believe about where we came from?" Absolutely. Our views on morality, justice, purpose, self-worth, humanity, obligation, and destination closely tie to our views on human origins. For example, without affirming or denying the veracity of the Evolutionary theory, let's take a moment to consider what the theory of evolution teaches about human origins and what impact this teaching has had upon human behavioral patterns.

What I have found is that evolution teaches that mankind has evolved over long processes of time, literally billions of years. The principle is that mankind has evolved from microscopic and simple life forms, from swamps and oceans then onto land and the apes, neanderthal man, and who we are today. I once heard someone put the concept into words this way, "from goo to you by way of the zoo!"

Evolution teaches that very clearly, there is no god, that you are a god. You can become a god, and that you make up your own rules. There are no other rules that God makes; you make up all your own rules. You do your own thing, and everybody can do whatever it is that makes them feel good. That's what the basic premise behind evolution is. There is nothing special about you; you are just another species in the evolutionary process. All that we see, including humans, developed in a purely materialistic, random way.

Evolution teaches that as species evolve, they eventually reach ideal population levels. As species advance, superior species eliminate inferior species -- "survival of the fittest." Weak and inferior members of a species should be eliminated to preserve superior bloodlines and for the conservation of essential resources. And since humans are merely a species of animal, we have no intrinsic value and are by no means exempt from the war of nature.

Let's apply the four questions and see how Evolution answers each of them:

1. Who am I? — You are a random process and chance animal species, which has evolved over long time periods, and your closest descendent are ape-like creatures.

2. Where do I come from? — You evolved by chance, and you are part of the evolutionary chain of events starting from swamps and bogs, then to oceans, to land, to apes to caveman to where you are today.

3. What is my purpose? — To survive, to grow stronger so you can defeat and eliminate the weaker beings around you. Your mission is to get all you can, when you can, how you can. It's all about you. You are the God of your life.

4. What happens when I die? — Your body is simply a mass of chemicals, and when you die, that's the end of it. There is no after-life, no hope beyond the grave.

Creation, on the other hand, teaches something very, very basic and much more positive. The Bible teaches in the very beginning that God had a plan for all of creation, including you. There was nothing random or evolutionary about it. With great love and intention, the Lord created the universe as we know it, the earth, the animals, plants, oceans, and the high point of all of it was to create human beings, man and woman.

Dr. Michael Denton, the author of *Nature's Destiny*, says this on page 389, "All the evidence available in the biological sciences supports the core proposition of traditional natural theology-that the cosmos is a specially designed whole with life and mankind as its fundamental goals and purpose, a whole in which all facets of reality, from the size of galaxies to the thermal capacity of water, have their meaning and explanation in this central fact."

You were created as a special, well-thought-out plan, the object of God's love for you. God knelt in the dust of the ground and formed our bodies, brain, and purpose with His very hands. Then finally, with His own breath, He breathed life into us. The human being was created by God's hands and made into His image and likeness. This reflects the great value that God would have a blueprint for us that is very similar to the blueprint of Him. It's very difficult to look around the world and not see overwhelming evidence for a Creator God in the external world. Every process of nature is orderly and deliberate. Our world reveals intelligent planning and a purpose. This is also evident in your internal world; your ability to love, your conscience, your ability to discover and reproduce are not the result of chance. All around you, the complexity of life can be seen and felt.

I believe that every single person reading this book is nature's greatest miracle. You are truly the high point of all creation. Since the beginning of time, never has there been another with your mind. Never has there been another created with your heart, your eyes, your ears, your hands, your hair, your mouth, or your personality. And there's never been nor will there be another that has your DNA. Think about that. None that have come before you, none that live today, and none that will come tomorrow can walk and think exactly like you. All of humankind are your brothers and sisters, yet you are different from each other. You are the high point of creation. You are nature's greatest miracle.

These same **four questions** have profoundly different answers from a creation intelligent design perspective as told in the Bible.

1. Who am I? — An intended creation, lovingly, fearfully, and wonderfully made, made in the image and likeness of the Creator of the Universe. (Psalm 139)

2. Where do I come from? — Created by God from the dust of the ground (Genesis 1:26-27)

3. What is my purpose? — To glorify God by using, sharing, and living each of your God-given talents, His created purpose for you, and love Him forever! (Roman 11:36, 1 Peter 4:11)

4. What happens when I die? — If you have accepted the Creator God as your Lord and Savior, then when He returns at His second coming, Heaven will be your reward. (1 Corinthians 15:51-55, Revelation 22:12)

That's why He looks at every person as very special, the high point of all creation. I love what Jesus Christ says in Matthew 6:26 (NKJV), "Look at the birds of the air, for they neither sow nor reap not gather into barns; yet your Heavenly Father feeds them. Are you not of more **VALUE** than they?"

The Bible describes a God who sees great value and worth in you because He created you to create, love, flourish, and have an amazing relationship with Him.

At the core of your existence is a uniqueness, individuality, distinctiveness that demands to be expressed. God has created in you all the potential abilities and powers we need to achieve our purpose, goals, and dreams. If there isn't something to be grateful for in all that, then call me crazy! We should all show our gratitude to the Creator of the universe for everything that is alive and exists, including the most important person ever created— **YOU.** In the next chapter, you will discover exactly how much potential you were born with and how miraculous you truly are.

Thinking About Life's Four Most Powerful Questions

If you were to view every person in your sphere of influence as having value and worth and made with intelligent design, how would that impact issues such as racism, class distinction, economic disparity, and political agendas?

The philosophy you adopt for your life, Evolution or Creation, determines all the outcomes of the four basic questions. Based on the view that you believe, how has that impacted and guided your life?

Which of the four questions in this chapter (and listed below for reference) gives you the most trouble to answer with conviction and why? How has that impacted your life to this point?

Who am I?

Where do I come from?

What's my purpose?

What happens when I die?

3

You Can Be a Superhero Because You Have Divine DNA!

"The potential of the average person is like a huge ocean uncharted, a new continent unexplored, a world of possibilities waiting to be released and channeled toward some great good."
Brian Tracy, author/coach

"What is man that You are mindful of him, And the son of man that You visit him? For You have made him a little lower than the angels, And You have crowned him with glory and honor."
Psalm 8:4-5 (NKJV)

What if you were created to do something of significance and great value during your life? The challenge is that many of the programs you received while growing up disguised themselves as truth; meanwhile, your true identity, potential, and purpose were hidden under the surface. Think about it this way, what if the programs you received in your childhood and as a young adult don't measure up to your intended purpose by the Creator of the universe?

A desire to achieve and excel is part of your design and was placed within you at birth. Unfortunately, during life's journey, you received so many of the wrong messages—messages that physically and chemically got wired into your brain— that you lost sight of the reason for your existence. But we all know deep down inside when we ask the question, "What is my purpose, why am I here?' you have a purpose and reason for being. You are motivated and emotionally moved to find out how to live your life with intention, purpose, passion, and belief.

Everything rises and falls on your belief that you have great value and an important meaningful purpose of fulfilling. There is a reason for you being here—and it's not just about living and dying, working, sleeping, and dealing with the ups and downs of life. You must believe you have an intentional job to do. The only way you will do it is to create new beliefs to override those negative programs that are not helping you; they were wrong.

Would it not be tragic if a very different, more vibrant you were buried under a pile of worldly to-do lists, expectations, and titles? Simply doing things because you felt like you should or need to. All because you mindlessly accept the world's expectancies of you? A life defined and directed from the **outside in** and not the **inside out**?

There is no greater stress than that generated by denying your true Bible-based identity. Because your life energy is being diverted and therefore depleted, you are compromised mentally, emotionally, spiritually, and physically.

There are several famous sports families that you would swear possess some sort of special athletic DNA. The Manning's in football, the Ripken's in baseball, the Bryant's and Curry's in basketball, and the Andretti's in auto racing, to name a few. It's as if they have some corner on the market with their blood-line. In reality, the children grew up in the best environment and were inherently passionate about what their parents did for work. They had the unique and special culture and background to succeed the same as their parents. I would say they were born to succeed and designed for greatness in their sporting fields. I believe that same premise goes for you as well.

The truth is you are born to succeed—every single one of us, no exceptions. You are designed with **Divine DNA,** which means you are created to excel. You are designed to grow, learn, overcome challenges, become stronger and better every day, and rise above the horrible place of mediocrity. You are created to reach the highest levels of personal growth and fulfillment. That's true for all of us. God does not play favorites. We all are created uniquely with equal opportunities for experiencing life to the fullest. God equips all of us with the tools, the ingredients, and everything we need. It is put there before you are born into this world.

The Miracle of YOUR creation as described by W. Clement Stone in his book, *Success Through a Positive Mental Attitude*:

"You are a very special person. And many struggles took place that had to be successfully concluded in order to produce the person we know as **YOU.** Tens of millions of sperm cells participated in a great battle, yet only one of them won—the one that made **YOU!** It was a great race to reach a single object: a precious egg containing a tiny nucleus. The head of each of the millions of sperms contained a precious cargo of 24 chromosomes, just as there were 24 in the tiny nucleus of the egg. Each chromosome was composed of jelly-like beads closely strung together. Each bead contained hundreds of genes to which scientists attribute all the factors of your heredity.

The chromosomes from the sperm from your Father, and the chromosomes from the egg from your Mother, contained all the material hereditary and tendencies from each of them. Your Mother and Father representing the culmination of thousands of years of victory in the battle to survive. And then one particular sperm, united with the waiting egg to form one, tiny living cell.

The life of the most important living person had begun, **YOU**. You became a champion over the most staggering odds you will ever have to face. Victory was built into you! No matter what obstacles and difficulties lie in your way, they are not one-tenth so great as the ones that have already been overcome at the moment of your conception."

Unfortunately, most of us don't see ourselves as special, as a champion created from the hand of God and having divine DNA flowing through our veins. We don't see ourselves as miracles of life, and, according to DNA scientists, no other person ever born or to be born will ever have your exact DNA makeup.

More commonly, people wrap their identity around three main areas: Personal Identity, Family Identity, and Social Identity.

Personal Identity consists of such things as your values and moral beliefs. It is how you see and feel about yourself. Your physical, mental, and emotional makeup. The way you talk to yourself and the impact of limiting beliefs on your life. The decisions you make, the goals set and achieved, and the successes, challenges, and defeats in your life.

Family Identity consists of family heredity, your unique generational characteristics and traits, your role in your family, and your mental and physical attributes.

Social Identity consists of peer acceptance or rejection, how well-liked you are by others, and how you fit into your community and society as a whole. Social identity also considers the influence of the working class, education, and financial achievement in your life.

One of more of these areas of identity significantly influences most everyone. And yes, they all play an important role in our growth as people, and all three identities influence us all to a certain degree. Ultimately, they are not the end game for you when it comes to your identity.

Growing up, all through school, my identity was wrapped up in my physical stature. As a boy, I was pretty close to the shortest kid in most of my grades and classes. I always felt I had to prove myself by being better at whatever I did than everyone else. I became very calculating and only participated in things I was good at and knew I could do better than most. I became a person filled with fears, especially the fear of failure. It was a hard way to grow up, especially knowing there seemed always to be someone better than me. I eventually grew to 5'7" and took up downhill skiing, a sport where being shorter in stature worked out much better mechanically for me.

It wasn't until I began to read the Bible where I started to see my identity had nothing to do with my size or stature. Especially after reading the example of Samuel as the Lord's messenger looking to anoint the next King of Israel after the failure of Saul. When he first saw David, he initially thought about his perceived limitations: his size, his age, his occupation, and his birth order. When all these things came to his mind, he felt David's brother Eliab should be anointed. Here is what God said to Samuel: "Do not look at his appearance or at his physical stature, because I have refused Eliab. For the Lord does not see as man sees; for man looks at the outward appearance, but the Lord looks at the heart." 1 Samuel 16:7

In God's eyes, the priorities are how we think, how we feel, how we learn from Him, obey Him, and glorify His name with our purpose, gifts, and talents. The world sees, how we dress, how we look, the cars we drive, what neighborhood we live in, the education we have, the church we attend, all these things from the outside matter. But God sees your identity in its purest and most perfect form because He personally designed and created you with purpose and intention.

Read the below Bible passages and really take in how they describe your creation and your identity:

Genesis 1:26-27: "Let us make man after our **image**, and our **likeness**."

How does it make you feel to know the God the Father, the Son Jesus Christ, and the Holy Spirit designed you after their image and likeness?

Genesis 2:7: "And the Lord God **formed man** of the dust of the ground, and breathed into his nostrils the **breath of life**; and man **became** a living being."

Is there something of great value you see in yourself when you understand the care, love, and imagination God put forth to literally form you from the dust of the ground?

How does it impact you seeing another person, knowing that they have God's breath of life in them?

Psalm 139:13-16: "For **You formed** my inward parts; You **covered me** in my mother's womb. I will praise You, for I am **fearfully and wonderfully made**; Marvelous are Your works, and that my soul knows very well. My **frame** was not hidden from You, When I was **made in secret**, and **skillfully wrought** in the lowest parts of the earth. Your eyes saw **my substance**, being yet unformed. In Your book they all were written, **the days fashioned for me**, when as yet there were none of them."

Your Creator, Lord God Almighty, cares for you so much that He made you in His image and likeness to be His child and to be His representative in this world. Think about how profound that is. It means that He created you with the ability to experience Him in a deep, intimate relationship. Likewise, He made it possible to pour His life into you and work through you in ways that will impact eternity. He desires that when people see you, they are reminded of Him and give Him glory. No matter how you feel about yourself, embrace the truth: You bear the image and likeness of the living God. You can know Him, walk with Him, and carry out His wonderful plans for your life with His power, wisdom, and leadership. God loves you, enables you, and works out His will through you.

When you look in the mirror, is it easy or challenging for you to say the words I am fearfully and wonderfully made? Do you feel special, or do you feel like you are telling yourself a lie? How are those responses impacting your life today?

Pondering being created in His image and likeness not only will bless your life but can absolutely transform the world in a way you never imagined possible.

I want to leave you with this thought as we wrap up this chapter on Divine DNA. Suppose you were created with everything you need inside of you to live an abundant, thriving for high achievement life. What could possibly keep you from reaching your goals and dreams?

The next chapter will help you tie in your created purpose so that you are amped up about the where and what of your life when you wake up every day.

Thinking About My Divine DNA

In the past, how have you typically identified yourself to others?

Has your life been typically defined and directed from the **outside in** or the **inside out**? How has that impacted your view of yourself and others?

Which of the three identities described in this chapter, personal, family, and social, has had the most profound impact on your life? How has it affected your relationships and your identity?

4

The Reason for Everything and WHY You Matter

"Without God, life has no purpose, and without purpose, life has no meaning, and without meaning life has no significance or hope."

Rick Warren, pastor and author of *The Purpose Driven Life*

Psalm 37:23-24: Follow the Lord's purpose for your life, you will not fail.

After reflecting on the previous two chapters, I hope you know there is a God who made you for a reason. Your life is not random or by chance but has a profound and significant meaning. You will discover that meaning and your intended purpose only when you make the Creator God the starting point of your life. As it states in Ephesians 1:18 (NKJV), "I pray that the eyes of your heart may be enlightened, so that you will know what is the hope of His calling, what are the riches of the glory of His inheritance in the saints."

The Ohsaki Study, conducted in Japan and included over 40,000 Japanese women and men aged between 40 to 79 years. Researchers focused on participants' level of purpose for their lives. They learned that those without a clear purpose had an increased risk of mortality in their life. The Ohsaki Study also found plenty of wellness benefits in the participants who said they have a purpose for their lives and living it. Here is a list of some of the positive outcomes:

77% rated their health as good or excellent
50% only experienced mild or very mild bodily pain
81% said they had unlimited physical functioning
69% consistently experienced sleep duration between seven and eight hours daily
22% stated that they experienced low levels of perceived mental stress

Living with purpose and understanding your WHY for your life has tremendous benefits physically, mentally, emotionally, financially, personally, and in your relationship with God. People who live without purpose get sick, diseased, depressed, fatigued, and unhappy. One of God's great gifts to us is living an abundant life and prospering in every area of our life once we have purpose and meaning, a calling higher than ourselves and our occupation. And that's what *Power to Thrive* is all about—helping you put the pieces together and creating a template for your life that will determine direction, relationships, income, and personal and work satisfaction. It's about thriving instead of just surviving. It's about experiencing joy and passion every day of your life, no matter what comes your way. It's about encouraging you and helping you to find your calling in this world so you can live a purpose-filled life.

You are who you are for a reason. God created you as part of a well-thought-out and perfectly designed plan. Everything about you is beautiful, perfect, and unique to you. Your physical traits, body, everything about the way you look are for a reason. God makes no mistakes, and you were fearfully and wonderfully made in your mother's womb. You are perfect just the way you are. Who raised you and that environment are part of shaping your heart for your intended purpose. The difficulties and trauma you have faced—though painful and life-changing— God will use to help shape your heart to accomplish His plan for your life. You are who you are, what you have experienced, everything you have gone through for a reason. You were formed by God's hand, not just to suck air and get by every 24 hours, but to really live with purpose, intention, and to give God glory.

When should you identify the path to find your God-given purpose?—when you're young, middle-aged, or older and wiser?

The answer is **NOW,** whatever your age. It's time to move forward, time to learn some new things, and it's your time to grow. If you are reading this, it's probably your time to align your God-given created purpose with the direction of your life. Maybe you need to review your past purpose or find a new direction. It's your time, and you are ready for that next step. You are ready to move forward; it's time for you to **THRIVE!**

In the Bible, you will very clearly find the personal mission of Jesus Christ and the Christian faith collectively. The mission of the Creator and Savior of the world was the following:

Luke 4:18-19: "The Spirit of the Lord is upon Me, Because He has **anointed Me**

to preach the gospel to the poor; He has sent Me to heal the brokenhearted,

to proclaim liberty to the captives and recovery of sight to the blind, to set at liberty those who are oppressed; to proclaim the acceptable year of the Lord."

- Preach the Gospel

- Heal the brokenhearted

- Set people free from sin

- Help people see their need of Him

- Give freedom to those oppressed

- To let people know the Messiah is here

That is what drove Jesus to get up every day. He knew why He was here, and everything He did revolved around that mission. He was anointed by God the Father and guided by the Holy Spirit to live for His intended and designed purpose.

Even the Christian faith has a great commission and a grand purpose. Jesus declared it to His followers just before He left them. It's clear, concise, and very intentional. Here is what Jesus said in Matthew 28:18-20: "And Jesus came and spoke to them, saying, "All authority has been given to Me in heaven and on earth. Go therefore and make disciples of all the nations, baptizing them in the name of the Father and of the Son and of the Holy Spirit, teaching them to observe all things that I have commanded you; and lo, I am with you always, even to the end of the age."

Later, in Mark 16:15-17, He said, "Go into all the world and preach the gospel to every creature. He who believes and is baptized will be saved; but he who does not believe will be condemned. And signs will follow those who believe."

- Take action and move

- Preach the Gospel to every person

- Make disciples everywhere they go

- Baptize people into a new life in Jesus Christ

- Teach them the things they learned from Jesus in the Bible

- Jesus Christ is with us through the Holy Spirit and He works through those who believe

The Christian faith is not about setting up camp here on earth; it's not about creating barriers and walls around certain beliefs. Jesus Christ Himself spells it out. The Christian faith is about moving and taking action. It's sharing the beautiful story of Jesus with others and helping them to grow closer to Him. We do this through obedience and commitment, participating in a new way of life, wiping the slate clean through baptism, and then allowing the Holy Spirit to use us. God's intended purpose is to use our gifts and talents to share God's love, His redemption, and His plan.

Having a grand and meaningful purpose for your life is the starting point of everything you want for your life. Think about a time in your life when you had something you were working towards that got you really excited. You jumped out of bed in the morning; it gave you energy, enthusiasm, initiative, creativity, discipline, and focus. There is nothing more powerful than a person who knows the WHY for their life and has a plan to accomplish it.

Unfortunately, today, most people, the majority actually, live their life with wishes, desires, and hopes. They don't really know their true purpose in life. People who are excited and understand God's purpose for them exercise belief, faith, have a passionate desire within them and a plan to accomplish it. They live life with intention and meaning.

If you feel disconnected from your pursuits—whether personal, professional, emotional, physical, or spiritual—it may not be that there is something wrong or inadequate about you, but that you are chasing the wrong things. Maybe you were told growing up what you were going to do with your life. Perhaps money, ego, or fame was the drive behind what you are doing today. Maybe you got a college degree and just settled after that. Perhaps you are married, and you feel trapped by having to provide for your family. Whatever it is, if it's not aligned with your created purpose in life, you will feel an emptiness inside of you.

When you are not aligned with your purpose, you will feel out of place, and that something isn't quite right. You may even feel physically sick, lack energy and well-being. You may have a negative mindset towards life due to your unhappiness with where you are. I know this for sure: God loves you. He made you and created you for a purpose. When you line up with His purpose, you feel the most incredible sense of peace, meaning, positivity, excitement, joy, and happiness every day you are alive. It's like the stars align, and you are living in the wheelhouse of life. You know you are right where you need to be and doing exactly what you are created to do.

The benefits of living with a definitive purpose for your life are powerful. Things like initiative, imagination, and enthusiasm become a reality for you. A clear purpose helps you better manage and discipline yourself with your time and money. You tend to stay more open to opportunities. You develop courage and faith in yourself and God. You make decisions based on your purpose and goal in life, not what others or society think you should do. You develop relationships with those who align with your mindset. You seek out those who can be part of your intended purpose. And most importantly, it helps you develop a mindset of success and vision for your life.

There are also tremendous health benefits from living out your purpose. According to a report in the February/March 2016 edition of *Psychosomatic Medicine: Journal of Biobehavioral Medicine*, people who possess a higher sense of purpose tend to live longer. Researchers reviewed ten studies involving more than 136,000 people to evaluate the relationship between purpose in life and the risk of death or cardiovascular disease. The participants, who were an average age of 67, were followed for about seven years. The risk of death was about 20% lower for people who reported still having a strong sense of purpose. They also had a lower risk of having a heart attack or stroke. The researchers speculate that a sense of purpose helps a person manage stress better and encourages a more active lifestyle.

"Just like people have basic physical needs, like to sleep and eat and drink, they have basic psychological needs," says Alan Rozanski, a professor at the Icahn School of Medicine at Mount

Sinai who has studied the relationship between life purpose and physical health. "The need for meaning and purpose is number one," Rozanski adds, "It's the deepest driver of well-being there is."

"Helping people cultivate a purpose in life could be an effective drug-free strategy to improve sleep quality, particularly for a population that is facing more insomnia," said Sleep Psychologist Dr. Jason Ong with Northwestern Medical Group.

In the Bible, God talked about purpose in Psalm 57:2: "I cry out to God most high, to God who will fulfill His purpose for me." And in Romans 8:28-31: "to those who are called according to His purpose."

Now it's time to help you find out what your created purpose may be. What has God planted in your heart that needs to come to fruition? Here are some questions for you to think about to help discover, dream, design, and discern your created purpose:

Why are you doing what it is that you do?

Is what you are doing with your life something that reflects and utilizes who you really are?

What do you wish you could put your whole heart into?

What impact do you want to have in this world?

What do you have a burning desire to accomplish in your life?

What would you be willing to sacrifice everything for?

What do you value most in life?

What are the beliefs and convictions that drive your life?

What is your dominant disposition and area of special giftedness?

What are you enthusiastic and passionate about?

What gets you excited to the point it changes your physiology and attitude?

What are your unique proficiencies and skills? What are you good at?

What are your unique identity and personality traits? What is your demeanor?

What has been your path in life: the good, bad, ugly, and beautiful?

How could you use your life experience or story to help others?

I want to ask you to do something right now that could radically change the direction and significance of your life from how you see it today. I have done this in my coaching practice with many people, and it's a game-changer for sure. You know the apostle Paul in the New Testament lived a purpose-filled life. He was only a short time from his execution by the Romans, and this is what he said about living for the Lord in 2 Timothy 4:6-8 (NIV), "For I am already being poured out like a drink offering, and the time for my departure is near. I have fought the good fight, I have finished the race, I have kept the faith."

How inspiring is it to come to the end of your life and know that you have lived your purpose and put everything towards its fulfillment! That's what God wants for you as well.

The average lifespan of a woman in the United States today is 81 years old. The average life span of a man is 77 years old. If you are healthy, eat well, exercise, take care of yourself physically, mentally, emotionally, and spiritually, you might add 8-10 years to your life. When you finish reading *Power to Thrive*, we will do that because you will desire to live the healthiest and best you.

I want you to think about how you want to finish your race of life on earth. As we all know, it's not so much how you begin or even run during the race; it's all about how you finish the race.

If you are a woman, take 89 and minus your current age. Put that number here____

If you are a man, take 85 and minus your current age. Put that number here____

Next, add that number to the year it currently is as you read this book, and that will give you the year you will die hypothetically. Obviously, you could pass away sooner or later, but this gives you a theoretical number to establish urgency and make plans.

How many years do you have left to live?_____

Now, to really put this into perspective, how many minutes, days, weeks, months do you have left to live? How many presidents will be elected? How many more times will you see your family every year? How many vacations do you have left if you take one to two per year? How many holidays or New Year's do you have left? Now that gets you thinking, doesn't it?

What is the vision for your life? The Bible tells us in Proverbs 29:18, "Where there is no vision, the people perish." By answering the questions in this book, you should begin to have clarity on your purpose in life.

Mark Twain once said, "the two most important dates in a person's life are the day they are born into this world, and the day they understand why."

In the next chapter, you will begin to understand the how and why of your decision-making process and how to determine what's really important in your life.

Thinking About My Purpose and WHY for My Life

Martin Luther King, Jr. quote, "Use me, God. Show me how to take who I am, who I want to be, and what I can do, and use it for a purpose greater than myself." How does this quote make you feel about your life?

What is your WHY? What is the reason for God creating you?

Is what you are doing in your life today incongruent with what you know you should be doing?

What's the one thing that you do that brings you more joy and happiness than anything else?

5

Finding the Moral Compass that Lives Inside of You

"Values are what we believe to be of the greatest importance and highest priority in our lives."
Hyrum W. Smith, author, founder of
Franklin Quest and Franklin Planner

"But the fruit of the spirit is love, joy, peace, forbearance, kindness, goodness, faithfulness, gentleness, and self-control..."
Galatians 5:22-23 (NIV)

The magnetic compass is one of the oldest and most essential navigation tools. Compasses are considered mandatory equipment for anyone venturing out into the wilderness. It's hard to imagine why hikers wouldn't bring one considering the ramifications of getting lost without any means of reorienting.

There are hundreds of thousands of stories of people trekking safely to their destinations without major incident thanks to planning, attention to detail, and proficiency with a compass and map.

For example, take the story of Waldemar Semenov during World War II.

A Nazi submarine ambushed the *SS Alcoa Guide* 300 miles off the North Carolina coast. The dire situation worried everyone onboard except for junior engineer Waldemar Semenov. With an almost inhuman stoicism, Waldemar collected himself, put on his best tie, gathered some supplies, and headed to the lifeboats. After three days in the open ocean, the crew used a small compass to navigate their way to a shipping lane, where a plane spotted them.

Semenov donated the compass to the National Museum of American History, along with this riveting account of his experience. He makes it very clear that without the compass onboard the lifeboat, they would have been lost and more than likely perished.

Values work this way too. Values supply you with a **moral compass** by which you navigate the course of your daily life. They are not conditional or situational.

Values make up what is **most important** in your life.

The truth is that **EVERYONE** has some value system they live by, that drives their behavior. Unfortunately for many, some of the values that drive behavior are contrary to inner peace.

Whether we realize it consciously or not, inner-values strongly influence our outward behavior. At the heart of each of us are some bedrock values and concepts that God gives to each of us. We were born with them. Then our parents, society, school, coaches, and pastors instilled values in us. These values make us who we are, and they influence how we approach the tasks of living.

Our natural inclination is for our actions to be consistent with these deeply held governing values. That's why we feel pain when our actions are inconsistent with our inner values.

Over time many of us allow our inner compass to diminish and the values of others, TV, movies, sports, church, politics, work, partying, alcohol, food, and gender (the word) to become more dominant on us.

We see two very different value systems in our world today. One based on Godly, Christian values, and the other termed many things such as secular, worldly, and post-modernism. Let's examine what matters most to adherents of the godly and the worldly value systems.

A worldly or secular value system tends to place a high value on the following areas:

Personal agenda guides your reality.

Life is valuable as it relates to you.

Your personal feelings define your reality.

You choose your own identity, and social approval is of high importance.

Profit and self-interest come first above all else.

On the flip side of the worldly value system is the Christian perspective on values. These are the values that are important to the Christian believer:

There is design and purpose in creation; the image of God defines us.

God decides who and what I am.

God determines the value of life.

God's code of conduct, His moral code, His Ten Commandments guide my reality.

Love for God and others is paramount.

Feelings have value but don't define truth.

God's approval matters most.

When you look at the lists of values for the Christian and Worldly perspectives, I hope you can see one very glaring difference between the two sets of values. The foundation for both of them comes down to the question of authority. The Bible asserts that God sets the standard about what's real and true and lasting;

the worldly perspective says that each of us gets to make up our own standards.

Now is an excellent time to take a moment and define what values are:

Values are enduring beliefs; defining a way of life, indicating what you care about. Values are your guide to life.

By identifying and clarifying your most important **values,** you can tap into your inner power to increase your effectiveness. You can focus on what's deep and meaningful to you. When our behavior is in line with our driving **values,** we experience inner peace.

Values are the actual parts of our lives that we think are so important that we stake our lives on them. We make great sacrifices to protect them or to help them grow. We must clarify what is most important in our lives and then decide to live by these values. Without values, there is confusion and chaos in our lives.

When values disintegrate, then everything disintegrates. When we pay attention to our values, order emerges out of the chaos of life. Many people's lives are out of balance today because of a lack of values. Many people have time management issues because they're not clear on what's important to them. They're not clear on their values, plain and simple, and your values control the direction of your life.

Do you have trouble making decisions? It's impossible to hit a target if you don't know what it is. Suppose you're having trouble making decisions in your life. In that case, it's often linked to the reality of what your values indeed are. If you're not clear on what's important in your life, you can't make decisions. When people have a crisis in their lives, those with clear values know what's important and can handle things quickly because their decision-making process revolves around their values.

Are you searching for inner peace?

> If you are the master architect of your own life, and
> you could create a set of values that would change
> your personal and professional life to be the best
> it could be, **what would your values be?**

I like how King Solomon emphasized living by Godly values in the Book of Proverbs. He spoke about it in many places; notice the following texts:

Proverbs 1:7: "the fear of the Lord is the beginning of knowledge, but fools despise wisdom and instruction."

Proverbs 4:25-27: "Let your eyes look straight ahead; fix your gaze directly before you. Give careful thought to the paths for your feet and be steadfast in all your ways. Do not turn to the right or the left; keep your foot from evil."

Proverbs 12:22: "The Lord detests lying lips, but he delights in people who are trustworthy."

Proverbs 21:3: "To do what is right and just is more acceptable to the Lord than sacrifice."

Go through the list of the possible values on the following pages and circle all the values that resonate with you. Don't think about it too much or overthink this exercise. Circle those values that make your heart stir and move your moral compass.

Abundance	Attractive	Comfort
Action-Oriented	Authenticity	Community
Adaptable	Balance	Compassion
Adventure	Benevolent	Confidence
Affection	Bold	Content
Affluent	Brave	Control
Ambition	Career	Cooperation
Approachable	Caring	Conservative
Articulate	Cheerful	Courage
Assertive	Choice	Courteous
Athletic	Christian	Creativity

Decisive	Health	Nurturing
Dedicated	Helpful	Obedient
Dependable	Honesty	Objective
Determined	Honorable	Open-minded
Diligent	Hospitality	Optimistic
Diplomatic	Humility	Order
Discernment	Humor	Organized
Discipline	Imagination	Original
Dynamic	Independence	Outstanding
Education	Innovative	Passion
Efficient	Inspiring	Patience
Empathetic	Integrity	Peace of Mind
Energetic	Intelligence	Perseverance
Enthusiastic	Intimacy	Personal Growth
Equality	Joyful	Persistent
Excellence	Justice	Personable
Family	Kindness	Planner
Fairness	Knowledge	Polite
Faithful	Leader	Politics
Fearless	Learner	Popular
Fitness	Legacy	Positive Attitude
Flexibility	Liberal	Power
Focus	Love	Proactive
Forgiveness	Loyal	Professional
Freedom	Making a difference	Punctual
Friends	Marriage	Purity
Frugal	Mastery	Purpose Driven
Fulfillment	Meaningful	Reliable
Fun	Memorable	Religion
Generosity	Merciful	Resourceful
Gentle	Meticulous	Respect
Giving	Money	Risk-taker
God	Motivated	Sacrificial
Gratitude	Neighborly	Security
Habits	Noble	Self-control
Happiness	Non-Conforming	Servant-hearted

Service	Tactful	Unique
Sex	Teamwork	Unity
Significance	Temperance	Virtuous
Sincerity	Thoughtful	Wealth
Spirituality	Thrifty	Wisdom
Strength	Tough	Work
Stability	Traditional	Worthy
Success	Trust	
Sympathetic	Understanding	

Next, review your circled values and narrow them down to your top ten. List them below, in any order. Just choose the ten most important and meaningful values to you.

_____   _____

_____   _____

_____   _____

_____   _____

_____   _____

Now take the ten values you chose and think about them carefully and thoughtfully. **Which one is your #1 value?** Which one is your #2? #3? Now order them from 1-10.

My Top 10 Values for My Life

1._____   4._____

2._____   5._____

3._____   6._____

7. _____   9. _____

8. _____   10. _____

Once you list your top ten values, write out what each value means to you. Identify what it means and why it is important to you.

Knowing and living your top values makes you more grounded, secure, confident, and decisive. Identifying your values will make it much easier to make those tough decisions. It will make it easier to say no to things that are not aligned with you. Your values should be entirely your own. You value what you think is deeply important and meaningful to you in your life.

Proverbs 11:3 (NIV): "The integrity of the upright guides them, but the unfaithful are destroyed by their duplicity."

In the next chapter, we begin to unravel the special gift God has created you with and how to put it to good use for the betterment of your community and the world as a whole.

Thinking About My Values

Up to this point in life, what has been the basis for your values—yourself, society, your culture, media, something else?

How much do you rely on your value system to guide you when you are making decisions?

How will your top ten values impact your life from this point forward?

How will things be different for you in your relationships, work, relationship with God, and finances if you allow your top 10 values to become your moral compass?

6

You are Created with Everything You Need for Greatness

*"When you find your spiritual gift, God will
give you an opportunity to use it."*
John C. Maxwell

"I wish that all of you were as I am. But each of you has your
own gift from God; one has this gift, another has that."
1 Corinthians 7:7 (NIV)

God created you with a particular intention and purpose for
this world. He knows exactly the role and part you are to play
as you interact with those around you, whether it's in your
family, local community, city, state, country, or internationally.
He planned exactly how He wanted you to serve Him. He gave
you the exact gifts, talents, and abilities to accomplish that task

and be the thriving person He designed you to be. That's what makes you so very unique and special; when you combine your special God-given gift with your one-of-a-kind DNA, you are indeed nature's greatest miracle.

Unfortunately, is that many people come to the end of their lives and still have not made the impact they intended or were created to make. Famous American Philanthropist Henry David Thoreau put it best, "Most men lead lives of quiet desperation and go to the grave with their song still in them." God's plan for you is that by the time you breathe your last breath and have sung your song, it has impacted many other lives.

A spiritual gift is a God-given ability placed into every individual when they are created. It is then activated when they become a Christian and receive the Holy Spirit's power. The primary purpose of these special gifts is to help you operate within your purpose and passion and bring glory and honor to the one who made you and gave the gift to you.

These gifts come in many different forms. Some gifts equip and build up people. Others are more supportive, and others more specifically geared to building up the Christian faith.

How can we find out what our gifts are? By doing the following three things:

1. *Pay attention to what stirs your heart.* If you are engaged in certain activities and find yourself filled with peace, joy, happiness, and higher energy, that could signal that those activities could be part of your purpose, passion, the reason for being, and the gift that God has given to you.

2. *By listening to what others are saying about you.* Often, we see ourselves in a more neutral or negative light, whereas others can see what we cannot. If you have numerous people telling you the same thing about your outcomes and the value you give, that may be a great sign you are touching people's lives.

3. *By taking a spiritual gift test to help determine your gifting.* There have been two prominent teachers in the area of spiritual gifts over the last 30 years. Dr. Larry Gilbert at www.church-growth.org has many materials online, and C.Peter Wagner also has an online spiritual gifts inventory test. Both have great information. Use the tests as a guide as you seek out your special gift from God.

After becoming a Christian when I was 24 years old, many great and faithful people discipled me for several years. They took me under their wings. I remember the day sitting in Bible Study class, and the teacher mentioned they were going to be gone the following week. They needed someone to teach class. They looked right at me and just stared. After a moment of awkward silence, I chimed up that I would do it for them. I studied like never before that week. I researched and dug deep into the Bible and other non-Bible resources. I came the following week to class very prepared. It went great. Before long, I was the primary teacher in the class, and the attendance kept increasing. After a while, people told me I had the gift of teaching, and I should consider evangelism. That went on for years until I got training and schooling and eventually became a full-time evangelist, teacher, and pastor of several churches in West Virginia. Sometimes you don't even know the gift buried deep within you. Still, when you begin to live by faith, taking action on promptings, getting out of your comfort zone, the Holy Spirit opens and reveals gifts to you. These are the very things that bring you peace, harmony, passion, and enthusiasm for benefiting those around you.

The primary scriptures that discuss spiritual gifts are 1 Corinthians 12, Romans 12:1-8, and Ephesians 4:7-16. As you look at the gifts included here, I want you to pay close attention to which ones resonate best with you. A good acid test, to begin with, is to ask yourself the question, *"Do I prefer to use my hands or to use my mouth."* Here is a list of special gifts God has given people to operate at their fullest potential, thrive, fulfill their destiny, and bring glory to Him. Circle those you know make you feel energetic, happy, and passionate. Then pick your top two that you know to apply to you.

Prefer to Work with Your Hands	**Prefer to Speak with Your Mouth**
Giving (time and money)	Teaching (research)
Apostle (spiritual leader)	Tongues
Faith (unwavering belief)	Interpretation of Tongues
Healings (help others sickness/disease)	Pastor (care for the church)
Miracles (humanly unexplainable)	Evangelist (speaking of God)
Mercy (care how others feel)	Prophecy (profess scriptures)
Leadership	Exhortation (encourage others)
Helps-Serving (doing for others)	Wisdom
Administration (orderly and organized)	Discernment of Situations/People
Ministry	Knowledge

I encourage you to recognize and know your gifts and know how to use them to build people up and magnify the Lord and the Christian faith. Paul said in 2 Timothy 1:6-7, "Therefore I remind you to stir up the gift of God which is in you through the laying on of my hands. For God has not given us a spirit of fear, but of power and of love and of a sound mind." We cannot let fear paralyze us. We must stir up and develop the gifts God has given us for His glory and for the benefit of helping people become the best that God created them to be. We must step out and live in them. We must embrace our gifts to achieve our dreams, live life with passion, enthusiasm, and the mindset to thrive. Not only will your life improve when you hone your gifts, but everyone who has a relationship with you or comes into your presence will also be improved.

Now, this is not as difficult as you may think it is. All it means is that you ask the Lord daily to guide your steps and show you how to serve Him. He will enable you to serve others in the way He created you—through your unique mix of personality, talents, and spiritual gifts. When you do, you will not only feel extraordinary joy and satisfaction in fulfilling your purpose in life but also God's pleasure. And this is something you don't want to miss!

The next chapter may be a challenge for you, especially concerning how you view God and how that impacts every area of your life. We will examine your view of Jesus Christ and your relationship with Him.

Thinking About My Special Gifts and Talents

How has discovering your spiritual gift changed your outlook on life and your relationships?

How will living your life in congruence with your special gift versus relying only on your talents, abilities, and your strength make things different for you?

What steps do you need to take now to embrace and live out your God-given gift the remaining days you have left on this earth?

List the steps below you will implement to make your special Gift from God more prominent and impactful in your life? By doing so, how will your life be different than it is now? How will your work, career, marriage, relationships, health, spiritual life, and community be impacted?

7

When You Look in the Mirror, Who Does God See?

"If you cannot hear the sound of the genuine in you, you will all of your life spend your days on the ends of strings that somebody else pulls."
Howard Thurman, author, theologian, civil rights leader

"Blessed be the God and Father of our Lord Jesus Christ, who has blessed us with every spiritual blessing in the heavenly places in Christ, just as He chose us in Him before the foundation of the world, that we should be holy and without blame before Him in love, having predestined us to adoption as sons by Jesus Christ to Himself, according to the good pleasure of His will, to the praise of the glory of His grace, by which He made us accepted in the Beloved."
Ephesians 1:3-6 (NKJV)

One of the most significant issues of identity today concerns how people see and view the character of God. In other words, His identity through your eyes. How your parents raised you and their ideas of God impacts how you see Him. Your experiences with religion, church, pastors, leaders, and whether you read the Bible for yourself or had other people tell you what it says. If you experienced some childhood abuse or trauma—or had a traumatic event happen to your family or friends—add to the identity you give God Almighty. People see God as energy, nature, distant, angry, mean, uncaring, the universe, and a supreme being.

From my ministry and professional coaching experience, I clearly see that our understanding of God is directly affected by how we relate to our earthly dads. Our first awareness of authority, love, provision, and security comes from our parents. It's only natural that how we perceive them would influence how we view all of our relationships, including and most importantly, the one we have with the God of the Universe.

The disciples of Jesus walked with him for three years. But even after all that time, they still struggled to understand God's character. We see this on one such occasion in John 14:8-9: "Phillip said to Jesus, 'Lord show us the Father, and that will be enough for us.' Jesus said to him, 'Have I been with you so long, and yet you have not known Me, Philip? He who has seen Me has seen the Father; so how can you say, 'Show us the Father'?'"

If you want to know who God is, look at the life of Jesus Christ. That means you can study the first four books of the New Testament, Matthew, Mark, Luke, and John. There, you will find the history of the life of Jesus and get an accurate picture of who God is. The way Jesus treats people is the way God treats us. What Jesus said to people is what God speaks to us. Jesus' attitude towards people is God's attitude towards us.

Most people see the Lord God Almighty as mean, angry, impatient, ready to zap us anytime we do something wrong, wanting to burn us in the flames of hellfire for eternity, responsible for this mess down here on earth, who fails all the time, who is responsible for all our challenges and bad things that happen to us, and so on. But if Jesus isn't like those things, then neither is our Heavenly Father.

God's character is based on one solemn truth throughout the Bible—God is Love! John tells us that God is love (1 John 4:8). That means if we know what love is, we can begin to get a picture of God's character. Thankfully the Apostle Paul gives us a fairly comprehensive definition of love as he writes a letter to the church in Corinth:

> Love is patient, love is kind. It does not envy, it does not boast, it is not proud. It does not dishonor others, it is not self-seeking, it is not easily angered, it keeps no record of wrongs. Love does not delight in evil but rejoices with the truth. It always protects, always trusts, always hopes, always perseveres. Love never fails. — 1 Corinthians 13:4-8

These are often the very words that many of us used in our weddings to express our love and commitment to our spouse. By extension, if God is love, here is what you can say about God's character:

God is patient.

God is kind.

God does not envy.

God does not boast.

God is not proud.

God does not dishonor others.

God is not self-seeking.

God is not easily angered.

God keeps no record of wrongs.

God does not delight in evil.

God rejoices in the truth.

God always protects.

God always trusts.

God always hopes.

God always perseveres.

God never fails.

Again, that is a very different picture of God than most people have in their minds. By understanding God's true character, it will allow you to see yourself through God's eyes. The Bible paints a stunning picture of how God really loves and cares for each of us individually and collectively as beings that He created. Let me paint that picture for you through the words of God Himself—

God says You are fearfully and wonderfully made and understood by Him...Psalm 139:1,13-15

God says You are created in His image and His likeness... Genesis 1:27

God says I made you a little lower than the angels and crowned you with glory and honor...Psalm 8:5

God says You are His workmanship created for good works...
Ephesians 2:10

God says You are a child of God and loved deeply by Him...
Galatians 2:20, 3:26

God says You are complete in Him...Colossians 2:10

God says You are chosen and blessed by Him...Ephesians 1:3-6

God says You are His special possession...1 Peter 2:9-10

God says You are more than a conqueror through Him...
Romans 8:37

God says You are a friend of Jesus Christ...John 15:15

God says You are not condemned by God ...Romans 8:1

God says You are forgiven completely by His mercy and compassion...Micah 7:14

God says You are forgiven as far as the east is from the west...
Psalm 103:11-12

God says You have been set free and redeemed through Jesus Christ...Ephesians 1:7

God says You are a new creation in Christ Jesus ...2 Corinthians 5:17

God says You have the mind of Jesus Christ...1 Corinthians 2:16

God says You are an ambassador for Jesus Christ...2 Corinthians 5:20

God says You are fellow citizens with the saints and members of the household of God...Ephesians 2:19

God says You are heirs of God and Citizens of heaven...Romans 8:17/Philippians 3:20

Wow! If that isn't awesome, I don't know what is. The Creator God of the Universe who made you, designed you, provided a way for you to be redeemed from the clutches of sin, wants to help you to thrive and live out your purpose in this life. He gives you every tool, skill, and talent needed to accomplish that. If God is for us, then what can come against us!

One of the most encouraging aspects of God's love for you is that He gives you supernatural power to live for Him. It's not your power or your strength; it's His power and strength working through us and in us.

The word "power" is in both the Old and New Testaments. The word in the Old Testament for power is *"koakh."* The word in the New Testament for power is *"dunamis,"* which is where we get the word dynamite.

In both the Old and New Testaments, Hebrew and Greek meaning for power means might, full of strength, abundance, miraculous power. This power is what God wants to give us if we will only let him. Notice how these scriptures tell you where power comes from—

2 Timothy1:7, "The Lord has not given us the spirit of fear, but power, love, and a sound mind."

Ephesians 3:20, "Now to Him who is able to do exceedingly abundantly above all that we ask or think, according to the power that works in us."

Luke 24:49, "Behold, I send the Promise of My Father upon you; but tarry in the city of Jerusalem until you are endued with power from on high."

If you want true power and the energy, explosiveness, and the magnitude of dynamite, then accept God's true character into your life. Allow yourself to look in the mirror each day and see yourself as God the Father sees you. Doing so will give you the *Power to Thrive*, escape the prison of mediocrity, tap into God's unlimited resources, and elevate your everyday living.

The next section of the book will examine your mindset—how and what you think about most often can turn your daily living into reality. Your outer world is a direct reflection of your inner world.

Proverbs 23:7 says, "For as he thinks within himself, so he is."

Thinking About Who I Am Through the Eyes of God

What has been your default belief about God in the past; how has that impacted your life and relationships?

How might your life be different if you adopted the true character of God and embraced the overall theme of the Bible, which is Love?

How have you been missing God's power in your life? If you allow God's power through the Holy Spirit to work in your life, what would be different for you?

PART TWO

Your Outer World is a Direct Reflection of Your Inner World

"You can't go back and change the beginning, but you can start where you are and change the ending."
C.S. Lewis, author and Christian theologian

Proverbs 23:7: As a man thinks, this is what he becomes.

8

The Greatest Gift Given to You by God

"Everything can be taken from a man but one thing; the last of the human freedoms—to choose one's attitude in any given set of circumstances, to choose one's own way."
Viktor Frankl, Austrian neurologist and psychiatrist, Holocaust survivor

"And if it is evil in your eyes to serve the Lord, choose this day whom you will serve, whether the gods your fathers served in the region beyond the River, or the gods of the Amorites in whose land you dwell. But as for me and my house, we will serve the Lord."
Joshua 24:15 (ESV)

W hen I was a young kid living in Phoenix, AZ, circa 1974, I was fascinated by Evil Knievel. I watched all his jumps on TV, read books about him, and had a doll and motorcycle set. I was so enamored with him. I loved to jump things on my bike. I would set up ramps and then see how far I could fly! This was about when Red Line and Mongoose were just coming out with their BMX line of bikes. I wanted one so badly. They had durable frames and special tires so you could do tricks and jump all day with them without damaging the bike.

My old bike took a beating and I needed a replacement. I told my parents over and over how much I wanted a Red Line or Mongoose bike so I could jump like my idol Evil Knievel. The challenge was new bikes were expensive—hundreds of dollars—with Red Line being the most expensive. My Dad worked full-time and went to school part-time at Arizona State University, working on his college degree. We were not poor by any means, but the fact was hundreds of dollars for a bike was not going to happen.

As Christmas approached, I lowered my standards to a Mongoose bike (not the Red Line) and put it on my list. Now my dad is a very handy guy and skilled with tools and cars. He modified my old bike with new welds in the most critical places, new handlebars, new tires, and a new paint job—red, white, and blue after Evil Knievel. On Christmas morning, I came out of my room, and I could not believe my eyes. I had never seen anything like it. It was so unique and cool- looking. It wasn't a Red Line or Mongoose, but in my eyes, it was even better! I rode that bike like a demon-possessed kid. I jumped tires, rocks, and dirt mounds. I challenged all my friends with Red Line and Mongoose bikes to jump-offs and usually won. I was so proud and grateful for that bike. That was the greatest gift I have ever received. I remember it shook my world. My Dad made it for me and designed it for me. He took the time to give me a bike I would love and be proud of—my greatest gift.

The question begs to be asked, what is the greatest gift God has given you? Maybe you think that it is your spouse, children, grandparents, education, money, home, sports, dancing, singing, or writing, and all of these are wonderful gifts. Still, none of them, yes I said it, none of them is the greatest gift given you by God.

What is the greatest gift given to you by God?

CHOICE…the most precious and awesome human freedom we have, a precious gift that has been given to us by God. That's where the **POWER** is for us. We are created as free, moral beings who make choices and exercise their free will. The direction of your life, moving towards goals and dreams, and charting a course for your life is entirely up to you.

Think about how profound and powerful this concept is. Instinct guides every other living creature on earth. They are unaware and without the capacity to even question. Out of all creation, God made you the high point of everything. He created you in His image and likeness. God gave you the ability to create your own life, think your thoughts, and behave how you want. Every day you put in place actions and ideas that will determine the shape and substance of your tomorrow. You can do this because of the greatest gift God has given to you.

The greatest gift God has given human beings is our ability to choose and make choices. The greatest power in the created universe is the power to choose! There is nothing outside of yourself that can hurt you. The Lord wants the best for you and would not hurt you. God loves you more than anything. The only thing that can hurt you is your own bad or poor choices. You hurt yourself by your unfortunate use of the great power God gave to us, the power to choose.

The suggestions of others have absolutely no power over you unless you allow them to. You give your mental consent by dwelling on what other people say and accepting their thought. At that point, it becomes your thought, and your subconscious mind works to bring it into your life as reality.

The bottom line is this:

You choose where to be ....You choose how to eat

You choose what to say................................. You choose what to do

You choose whom to be with...............You choose what you focus on

You choose what to believe.................... You choose when to go along

You choose when to resist..........................You choose whom to trust

You choose whom to avoid .... You choose how you dress

You choose how to respond or react ......You choose to have faith or not

Because we make all of these choices, we must accept responsibility for our life. There is only one person responsible for the quality of the life you live today; that person is **YOU**. **Suppose** you want to be successful in life. In that case, you have to accept responsibility for your level of achievements, your results, the quality of your relationships, the state of your health both physically and mentally, your income, finances, and your feelings—yes, everything!

As a human being, the struggle is real. We never want to look at where the real problems lie, which 99% of the time is **YOU**. We love to blame, play the victim, for what's happening or where we have ended up in life. We blame our parents, childhood, teachers, coaches, pastors, clergy, church, bosses, coworkers, family, siblings, spouse, the media, the weather, the economy, lack of money, or a lack of resources…does this sound familiar to you? The truth is that you must take personal responsibility for your life—everything. Nothing can change the past or what may have happened to you, but you can change yourself at this very moment. You have the power to make a choice, decide to move forward, and stop looking back.

My good friend and insurance business coach from 8% Nation, Cody Askins, likes to say this about excuses, "We don't' make them, and we don't listen to them. You can use moving, pandemics, illness, weather, relationships, environment as excuses for why something might not work out for you, but the thing about excuses is that it's usually something you say that makes you feel better about your mistakes or failures." If you want your life to be better and move forward, you need to stop making excuses for your actions, decisions, or place in life. Accept responsibility and move on.

Directly tied into personal responsibility is an attitude and mindset of complaining. When you complain, it means that you believe that something better exists. Whether you complain about money, career, marriage, relationship, health, where you live, or *whatever* is on your mind, you have an image of something better in mind, that you prefer. But, you are unwilling to take the risks required to create it.

The Bible says this about complaining in Philippians 2:14, "Do all things without complaining and disputing, that you may become blameless and harmless children of God." And Ephesians 4:29 says, "Let no corrupt word proceed out of your mouth, but what is good for necessary edification, that it may impart grace to the hearers."

You only complain about things you can do something to change. You need to either accept that you choose to stay where you are or take responsibility for your choices and stop complaining. Take the risk that is necessary to create your life exactly the way you want it. Bottom line, either take action to make the necessary change or decide to stay mediocre, average, and unhappy.

If you want to create a thriving, powerful life—the life of your dreams—then you must take 100% personal responsibility for your life. As you read this page, starting right now, make a vow to give up all your excuses and all your victim mentality. Let go of all the reasons you can't and why you haven't up to now, especially blaming outside circumstances. It's time to throw them all away and burn your ships in your life, and don't look back again.

Here is what the Bible says about being a responsible person in Ezra 10:4, "Arise, for this matter is your responsibility. We are also with you. Be of good courage, and do it." In Galatians 6:4-5, it says, "But let each one examine their own work, and then he will have rejoicing in himself alone, and not in another. For each one will bear bearing his own load."

When you stop and think about it, you only have control over three things in your life: the thoughts you think, the images you visualize, and the actions you take. How you use these three things determines everything you experience in life. Period; it is that simple. It all begins with the power to choose—the Creator of the Universe, empowered you with this amazing gift!

As you will see in the next chapter, your ability to grow, develop, and change is really about your mindset and whether it's in a fixed or growth mode.

Thinking About My Greatest Gift Given to Me by God

How have excuses and victim mentality shaped your world and the outcomes in it?

What choices and decisions have you made that maybe did not turn out well, but you still haven't accepted responsibility for them yet?

What are the consequences—the relationship damage, the lack of promotion or financial gain, etc.—that you are making excuses for?

What is something in you know could be better in your life, but all you have been doing is complaining about it? What steps can you take right now to make that situation better?

How do you see your life becoming more powerful if you hold yourself accountable and embrace the wonderful gift that God has given you to make better choices and decisions?

9

Mindset is More Important than Talent or Ability

"For twenty years, my research has shown that the view you adopt for yourself profoundly affects the way you lead your life. It can determine whether you become the person you want to be and whether you accomplish the things you value."
– Carol Dweck, author of *Mindset: The New Psychology of Success*

"For as he thinks in his heart, so is he."
Proverbs 23:7 (NKJV)

Let's start discussing mindset by considering two questions:

Question 1: Can your intelligence and personality be developed, or is it a fixed, deep-seated trait?

Question 2: Are mindsets a permanent part of your makeup, or can you change them?

Experience, training, and personal effort can take you to another level of personal development. The view you adopt for yourself can profoundly affect how you lead your life and the person you are created to be. You will discover that mindsets are just powerful beliefs and that the brain is like a muscle; it can change and become stronger the more you use it and learn.

The science of neuroplasticity studies your brain's ability to continually change itself—who you will become and how successful you'll be, will be less up to your upbringing or the circumstances of your life, and more up to the wiring you decide to create in your brain. Neuroplasticity is the brain's ability to re-organize itself, both physically and functionally. The message of neuroplasticity is that the brain can change!

Science proves to us today that every created being, whether in South America, Africa, India, China, Russia, Iraq, Ireland, Canada, Mexico, United States, has the capacity for lifelong learning and brain development. It doesn't matter whether you are rich or poor, born into privilege or in the slums, whether you have white, black, red, yellow, or brown skin, or what your IQ or SAT scores are—you can grow, learn, and become the person you want to be. Nothing is set in stone. If you choose to become the person God created you to be, then none of the above factors should hold you back.

Experience, training, and effort can take people to a higher level of personal development. The view you adopt for yourself profoundly affects how you lead your life and the person you want to become.

In my family, where my father was the first person in his family to graduate from college, going to college was emphasized a lot in our home. My sister has her master's degree. My daughter has her master's degree as well. For some reason, going to college had minimal appeal to me. I consider myself a self-made man. I have developed myself over the years through reading hundreds of books and attending seminars and workshops on personal development, self-help, sales, business, health, money, relationships, spiritual things, etc. I have lived a very diverse and interesting life with my occupations. I have become an author, a business owner, a business and life coach to others, a Senior Pastor, and an evangelist. Though I have made plenty of mistakes and poor choices that had negative consequences, I don't see myself as any less or any better than someone who has a college degree or higher education. My education came through the belief that I could become and be whatever I wanted to be, learn and develop new skills, and teach myself through experience how to do the things that would bring me to where I am today.

I tell you this because I felt very guilty and inferior for years because I did not have a college degree. I had this fixed mindset that I could only become so much of what I wanted to be without a college education. Now, I can see my path was the right path for me. It's not for everyone for sure, but don't allow yourself to be in a box that tells you if you do this or don't do this, you will become this. As long as you have a growth mindset and an open mind to self-study, you can do and become whatever you set your mind to. I have embraced Napoleon Hill's famous phrase and success trait, "Whatever the mind can conceive and believe, it can achieve."

Remember, you can choose, and our mindsets are just powerful beliefs. A person's mindset is more powerful than their talent. Our brain is like a muscle that changes and gets stronger the more you use it and learn. What's even more exciting is that you can do things to produce effective brain change and growth. Things like focus, diet, relaxation, daydreaming, reading, and holding negative or positive thoughts can change the brain for good or bad.

I've compiled a list of ways that you can keep your neuroplasticity growing and your mind ever-expanding:

1. Stay curious and always keep learning.

2. Having a definite major purpose and a big WHY for your life.

3. Exercise and move daily.

4. Get out of your comfort zone, learn new things, and take risks.

5. Meet new people every week and engage in conversations.

6. Try not to multi-task; instead, be focused on one task at a time.

7. Challenge your old beliefs and seek new perspectives.

8. Daily devotional, prayer, and Bible study.

9. Be a strategic thinker and always look for ways to improve things.

10. Develop new and different habits and mix things up in your life. Variety can be good.

Two schools of mindset exist, growth and fixed, each with its own severe and profound consequences. The mindset you adopt will lead you to certain outcomes and potential for your life. Suppose you believe that no matter what befalls you, God has given you the ability to continually develop your intelligence, personality, and education. In that case, you will have specific definite outcomes based on that mindset. Likewise, if you believe intelligence, personality, and education is a fixed, deep-seated trait, unmovable and unexpandable. In that case, you will have definite outcomes based on that mindset too.

One of the biggest myths thrown around for years in the self-help industry—although thoroughly debunked now—is the idea that *humans only use 10% of their actual brain capacity*. This is not true at all. The human brain is very complex and difficult to comprehend fully, but the idea that 90% of your brain is just wasted space is entirely false. I believe the reason this myth exists is that people are confusing brain usage with human potential. Most of you reading this book know that you can achieve so much more than you do. You can reach goals and dreams, and to do so would not require our using the brain's potential power but understanding how to use our brain better. With magnetic resonance imaging, scientists now can see how active the brain is all the time. The truth is that you use virtually all your brain every day! That's why understanding how your mind works can increase your effectiveness many times over to help you reach your God-given potential and possibility.

When you pro-actively take charge of your mind, you ultimately will take charge of your life. When you understand your thoughts, feelings, emotions, beliefs, and desires, you can direct them toward your purpose and accomplish your goals. True wisdom comes from taking the time to study and know yourself, to know *why* you are the person you are. Taking charge of your mind is a thoughtful, reflective, daily, solitary process. Only you can come to understand the complex inner workings of your mind. You must be willing to spend the time and effort that gaining such insight requires to be the incredible creation that God always had in mind for you.

To help you gain further insight, let's look at the beliefs and principles behind both the growth and fixed mindset.

Growth Mindset Beliefs and Principles

Based on the belief that your basic qualities are things you can develop through your efforts, everyone can grow through application and experience. A person's true potential is unknown and, most of the time, untapped.

Definition of Success: Did I learn something new today to make myself better? Am I expanding my horizons so I can challenge myself to be the best God created me to be?

- Has a passion for learning and development
- Emphasis is on getting better, making improvement
- Founded on the belief of change, things can be different if you want them to be
- Overcoming deficiencies and open to self - evaluation
- Know very well their strengths and weaknesses
- Stretch and challenge yourself to grow, thrive on it
- Getting out of your comfort zone, feel the fear, and do it anyway!
- Using adversity and defeat as a stepping stone to growth
- Willing to take risks to grow, not afraid to fail or be defeated
- Failure is viewed as action or one time happening, doesn't define you
- Whatever the mind can conceive and believe, it can achieve
- Everything is about the journey, not the outcome
- What can I learn from my past experiences, and how can I grow from them?
- Internal monologue is not about judging one's self or others

In modern psychology and therapy, the principle of a growth mindset mentality is the primary focus. According to Dr. Martin Seligman, who is seen as the foundational force behind **positive psychology**– the positive psychology movement can be described as:

The study of what constitutes the pleasant life, the engaged life, and the meaningful life. It is the scientific and applied approach to uncovering people's strengths and promoting their positive functioning. Positive psychology is about flourishing. We flourish when we cultivate our talents and strengths, develop deep and meaningful relationships, feel pleasure and enjoyment, and make a meaningful contribution to the world.

Positive psychology, in a nutshell, is a scientific approach to studying human thoughts, feelings, and behavior with a focus on strengths instead of weaknesses, building the good in life instead of repairing the bad, and taking the lives of average people up to "great" instead of focusing solely on moving those who are struggling up to "normal."

Positive psychology focuses on the positive events and influences in life, including:

1. Positive experiences (like happiness, joy, inspiration, and love)

2. Positive states and traits (like gratitude, resilience, and compassion)

As a field, positive psychology spends much of its time thinking about topics like *character strengths, values, optimism, overall life satisfaction, happiness, a person's well-being, gratitude, compassion (as well as self-compassion), self-esteem, self-worth, self-confidence, and hope.*

Fixed Mindset Beliefs and Principles

Based on the belief that your qualities are carved in stone. You only have a certain amount of intelligence, personality, and moral character. Creates an urgency to prove yourself.

A fixed mindset believes that 65% of your success is from ability and 35% is from the effort.

Every situation is evaluated by questions such as: Will I succeed or fail? Will I look smart or dumb? Will I be accepted or rejected? Will I feel like a winner or a loser? The frequent phrase of a fixed mindset is "I can't do it."

Definition of Success: establishing their superiority, pure and simple. They are worthier and more special than everybody else…everything rises and falls on talent.

- Fear challenge

- Devalue effort, it's a bad thing, means you're not smart or talented

- You can learn new things, but you can't really change how intelligent you are

- You are a certain type of person, and you really can't change that

- Concern about how you will be judged by others

- Supersensitive about being wrong and making mistakes

- Proving your smart or talented, validating yourself

- Thrive on staying in and feeling safe and secure in a comfort zone

- One test or one evaluation can measure you forever

- Failure is viewed as an action that affects my identity

- Tend to believe in victim and blame mentality, fear of failure

- Everything is about the outcome

- Stands in the way of development and change

- There is something in your past that measures or defines you

- Has an internal monologue that is focused on judging

The bottom line is this, how you view yourself has a massively positive or negative effect on the way you lead your life and the person you want to be. Your mindset will impact every area of your life, from career and work success, healthy relationships, income levels, financial prosperity, education, and what you do and become in your everyday life. That's how important your mindset really is.

In the next chapter, we will uncover the single greatest deterrent to your personal success and how to break through it and help you become bulletproof when trying new things or getting out of your comfort zone.

Thinking About My Mindset

Which mindset seems to be the one ruling and directing your life today? How has that impacted your life?

What lies have you allowed to define who you are?

Why is it easier for you to focus on the negatives in your life than the positives?

Purchase the book *Strengths Finder 2.0: Discover Your Clifton Strengths* by Tom Rath and Don Clifton. It will help you identify your top five positive strengths in your life. When you focus on those things, you do well and allow yourself to thrive.

10

Existing in the Death Zone of Life

"I can honestly say that nothing good in my life has ever happened from the safety of my comfort zone. It's all those moments where you feel challenged, where you think 'Oh crap, maybe this wasn't such a good idea' and then ponder giving up – if you can get through this stage of doubt and make it out the other side – I promise you, this is where the good stuff happens."
Richard Branson, entrepreneur, investor, author, and philanthropist

2 Timothy 1:7: God has not given me the attitude or feelings of fear, but created my mind to be filled with courage which gives me power to do all things through Him, and to use my mind to love others, and to be disciplined in our thoughts and actions.

Mount Everest is the highest mountain in the world. Its summit is 29,029 feet — or 5.5 miles — above sea level. Climbers and scientists have a special name for the highest part of Everest, everything above 26,247 feet (8,000 meters): "The Death Zone." At this level on the mountain, oxygen is 34% the concentration it is on the ground below. The body's cells start to die, minute by minute and cell by cell. Climbers' judgment becomes impaired. They can experience heart attacks, strokes, or severe altitude sickness. The climbers are racing against the clock of their bodies breaking down and essentially dying.

Over the last few years, climbers' lines and wait time to reach Everest's summit have been so long that climbers in the Death Zone are dying of exhaustion waiting in line for their turn to climb. Human bodies work best at sea level. Down here, oxygen levels are adequate for our brains and lungs. At much higher altitudes, our bodies cannot function properly.

Just like The Death Zone on Mount Everest, we have a zone we can live in that can be a human killer. When you live in the "Comfort Zone" of life, you experience fear, contentment, mediocrity, just getting by, playing it safe, being like everyone else, insecure, procrastinating, and regret. It's a place in human existence you are not meant to live in for very long. If you spend too much time here, you begin to die mentally, emotionally, physically, spiritually, and financially.

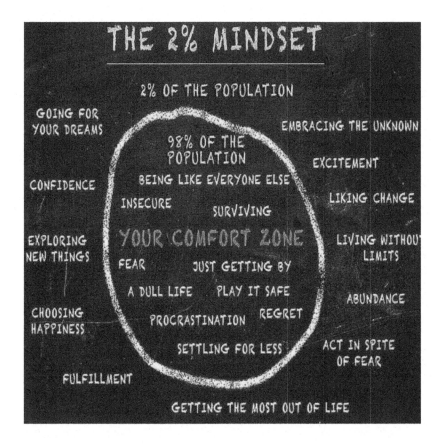

Your comfort zone is a **self-created prison**. It consists of your limitations, a collection of can nots, musts, must nots, and other limiting beliefs formed from all your negative thoughts and decisions you accumulated and reinforced during your lifetime. The challenge is that you have to get out of and break through that comfort zone to be able to thrive in life. Famous author Jack Canfield puts it best by saying, "Everything you want in life is on the other side of fear."

The challenge comes when we begin to push through our comfort zone. At that moment, we begin to experience fear and anxiety because it's new and uncomfortable. You're sending your brain new messages and ideas for it to act upon. I always tell my coaching clients if they feel uncomfortable, that's a good sign they are moving out of their comfort zone.

Every successful person I know has been willing to take a chance, a huge leap of faith, despite the fact they were scared out of their minds, literally! But they also knew if they didn't take action, the opportunity would pass them by. They felt the fear, knew they could handle it, and did it anyway. Every time you explore new things or try something out for the first time, you feel uncomfortable. But if you are going to go for your dreams, be truly happy, embrace the unknown, live a life of abundance and fulfillment, truly living life without human limits, you will need to venture out beyond your comfort zone. Nothing great happens when you are in the death zone of life, we call the comfort zone.

Let's dive deep here and explore what fear and anxiety are really about and how to live your life not being controlled by them. Fear can be one of the greatest killers of success and stop you from living a *Power to Thrive* life.

Whenever we start something new and different, when we take a big risk and put ourselves out there, we will usually experience some level of fear. Unfortunately, most people let fear stop them from taking the necessary steps to achieve their dreams.

What is fear?... an unpleasant, often strong emotion caused by anticipation or awareness of danger likely to cause pain or a threat, whether the threat is real or imagined.

There are two kinds of fear, according to the Bible. Constructive fear, which is how we honor God, such as "fear the Lord" or "fear God," is referenced throughout the Bible. It means to respect His authority and revere Him. Destructive fear tends to be very negative and impacts us in ways God did not intend. Things like paranoia, phobias, anxiety, terror, panic, unbelief, and limiting beliefs come from this second type of fear.

The Bible actually refers to fear as a form of slavery; when a person experiences fear, they can become paralyzed and stuck from taking action or making important decisions. The scripture says in Romans 8:15, "For you did not receive the spirit of slavery to fall back into fear, but you have received the Spirit of adoption as sons, by whom we cry, 'Abba! Father!'"

When we even hear that word today, slavery brings horrible scenes of abuse, mistreatment, and unfairness to our minds. The actual definition is disturbing enough:

"Slavery and enslavement is when someone is forbidden to quit their service for another person and is treated like property. Slavery relies heavily on the enslaved person being intimidated either by the threat of violence or some other method of abuse."

That, my friend, is the incredible danger and awfulness of what fear does to us. It allows us to give up our God-given power over to the devil himself, to be intimidated by forces of nature that are not of God's making. Fear brings with it mental, emotional, and physical abuse to a person's very own soul.

Another very negative aspect of fear that affects us comes from the Apostle Paul in the New Testament in 1 John 4:18 (ESV), "There is no fear in love, but perfect love casts out fear. For fear has to do with *punishment*, and whoever fears has not been perfected in love." I think most of you can relate to this powerful truth. Fear is punishing; fear is mental anguish at its worst.

Other than the Bible itself, the best book I've read about dealing with fear is by Dr. Susan Jeffers called *Feel the Fear and Do it Anyway!* The key phrase throughout her book was this: **Feel the fear and do it anyway!**

Two of the most destructive forces in the human mind are **fear and anxiety.** If you are constantly tired, stressed, emotionally flat, depressed, worried, and unhappy, then you are not living your God-designed purpose and are just going through the motions. Maybe you aren't as sharp as you once were and find yourself more cynical, apathetic, filled with hopelessness, or lacking optimism. More than likely, this is happening to you because you have abandoned your true self and what matters to you. Anxiety is the result of me envisioning my future without the Lord God Almighty!

Don Joseph Goewey, noted author of the book *The End of Stress* and managing partner at ProAttitude, says this about his study on stress and anxiety:

"85 percent of what subjects worried about never happened, and with the 15 percent that did happen, 79 percent discovered either they could handle the difficulty better than expected, or the difficulty taught them a lesson worth learning. This means that 97 percent of what you worry over is not much more than a fearful mind punishing you with exaggerations and misperceptions."

Think about how much mental, emotional, and physical energy you exert worrying about things that most likely never happen? How much precious time do you spend worrying? What a terrible way to live your God-given life—At the end of your life, you come to the end and realize, 97% of what you worried about never happened.

I heard a story about an elderly monk. He was training several younger monks and teaching them to live service-oriented lives. One of his pupils came to him and told him that he was so weighted down with all of his worries that he could not perform his tasks. The old, wise monk said, "I have a gift for you. It was given to me by an old and wise monk when I was your age. This gift has allowed me a life of grace, peace, and focus."

At that point, the older monk handed the young man a worn and battered wooden box with a small slot cut into the lid. The young man barely disguised his doubt when he asked, "What possible good could a box like this do to help me alleviate all of the worries in my life?"

The wise old man explained, "This box is a tool. Like any other tool, in the hands of someone who knows how to use it, it is most useful and effective." The old man explained that the purpose of the box was to hold all of one's worries. When confronted with any trouble, problem, or worry throughout the week, the old monk would simply write down the issue at hand on a slip of paper and put it into the box. Then, once a week, he would dedicate a morning to going through the slips of paper accumulated throughout the week. After 40 years of pursuing this practice, the old monk discovered that most problems and worries solve themselves long before the week is out.

Problems and worries fall into three categories: 1. those that we can do nothing about, 2. those which resolve themselves regardless of our worry, and 3. problems or worries that we can directly affect with our actions. The third type is the problems we should focus our energy on. Dedicating our energy to them will turn these unproductive worries into productive areas of our life.

Focus and action are the keys. Like the monk, take the worries out of your daily life, and schedule them in once a week. Take your concerns and act upon them immediately.

Jesus says in Matthew 6:27, "Which of you by worrying can add one cubit to his stature?" Amazingly, almost all of your fears are now self-created by imagining some negative outcome in the future.

Most psychologists describe fear as:

*F*antasized

*E*xperiences

*A*ppearing

*R*eal

Many fears are often born from a desire to control the outcome rather than trusting in obedience to God. The foundation to all your fears, according to Dr. Jeffers, is: **"I can't handle it."** As a matter of fact, in the Bible alone, there are constant references to angels and messengers of the Lord who say the same thing to those they appear to—"fear not." Let's look at some of the great examples in the Bible on this topic.

Before Joshua took on the monumental task of entering the promised land with the children of Israel, the Lord God Almighty says this to him in Joshua 1:9: "Have I not commanded you? Be strong and courageous. Do not be frightened, and do not be dismayed, for the Lord your God is with you wherever you go." In other words, God was saying to Joshua, "You can handle it. You can do this thing I have asked of you. Trust My Word."

One of the greatest best biblical examples of fear would be the story of Gideon. This man God chose to be a leader amongst God's people and rescue Israel. God reaches out to him when he is hiding in a winepress to escape his enemies (Judges 6:11). The Bible indicates that Gideon demonstrated fear, anxiety, and doubt through most of this story. He constantly tested God by asking him to perform signs. Whether it was performing some sign with food, a fleece, or asking God numerous times to perform the same sign, he had God consume an offering of food he presented to the angel (Judges 6:20-40).

Gideon was very afraid of what God was asking him to do, but when he finally put his trust in God and obeyed, the Israelites had their freedom after seven years of oppression.

In other words, God was saying to Gideon, "You can handle it. You can do this thing I have asked of you. Trust My Word."

Later, in Judges 7:1-7, when Gideon was leading 32,000 troops against the Midianites, God told Gideon he has too many wrong mindset people to go into battle. His first test is found in verse 3, "Whoever is fearful and afraid, let them turn and depart at once from Mount Gilead…and 22,000 of the people returned." Eventually, he got down to 300 warriors who would fight and defeat the Midianites.

In other words, God was saying to Gideon, "You can handle it. You can do this thing I have asked of you. Fear is not to be part of this battle. I will deliver your enemy into your hands. Trust My Word."

When God is assuring Israel of His help as they rebuild and recommit to Him, He says this through the prophet Isaiah in Isaiah 41:10, "Fear not, for I am with you; be not dismayed, for I am your God; I will strengthen you, I will help you, I will uphold you with my righteous right hand."

In other words, God was saying to Israel, "You can handle it. You can do this thing I have asked of you. Trust My Word."

And look at the Apostle Paul, a man who experienced things many of us cannot relate to, who was in situations which must have been scary beyond belief. He had his eyesight taken from him for a while, and he was stoned. In addition, he was in life-threatening storms, shipwrecked, starved, imprisoned, hated, plotted to kill by his friends and religious family, beat up by a mob, bitten by a poisonous snake, beaten with rods, practically homeless, many times cold and naked, sleep-deprived, and robbed. And we think we have it bad some days?! This man was indeed the New Testament Forrest Gump! Can you imagine the level of fear Paul had to deal with in his life, almost daily, sharing the Gospel of Salvation thru Jesus Christ? And yet, what does he say in Hebrews 13:6, "So we can confidently say, 'The Lord is my helper; I will not fear; what can man do to me?'"

In other words, God was saying to Paul, "You can handle it. You can do this thing I have asked of you. Trust My Word."

There will always be moments in life when we are worried about giving ourselves over to God, but the truth is we can trust him with our tomorrows. Obedience does not require us to be fearless; it only asks that we have the faith to follow God when an opportunity arises or overcome a challenge. That's why we can say with the utmost confidence as the Apostle Paul said in Philippians 4:13: "I can do all things through Jesus Christ who gives me strength."

You are either running from your fears (which means they have power over you), or you are embracing your fears (which means that you have the power over them). When we can get to a place where we are comfortable *"dancing"* with fear, then your life will never be the same. Fear is not something to be afraid of; it's something that you create in your mind, so the new mantra to live by is this:

*F*ace

*E*verything

*A*nd

*R*ise

When you take God at His Word and place your trust in Him, you can rise far above any destructive fear. God's word, the Bible, which is truth + trusting in the Lord who has not given you the spirit of fear = *Power to Thrive*.

Remember the words in Philippians 4:6-7, "Do not be anxious about anything, but in every situation, by prayer and petition, with thanksgiving, present your requests to God. And the peace of God, which transcends all understanding, will guard your hearts and your minds in Christ Jesus."

Identify Your Fears

Circle the fears below that apply to your life.

Fear of Poverty	Fear of Loneliness
Fear of Criticism	Fear of Being Unloved
Fear of Poor Health	Fear of Disappointment
Fear of Loss of Love	Fear of Being Judged
Fear of Old Age	Fear of Change
Fear of Losing Your Freedom	Fear of Being Embarrassed
Fear of Death	Fear of Rejection
Fear of Failure	Fear of Life's "What If's"
Fear of Success	Fear of Being Overwhelmed
Fear of Looking Foolish	Fear of Taking Action
Fear of Public Speaking	Fear of Making Mistakes

Fear of Being Hurt

Fear of Losing Everything

Fear of Not Being Good
Enough

Fear of Not Being Smart
Enough

Fear of Circumstances

Fear of What Others Think

Fear of Complacency

Fear of Not Having
Enough Time

Fear of Loss of Self

Fear of Being a Fraud

Next, put a checkmark beside your top three fears. Last, put them in order from 1-3. Now you can look your nemesis straight in the eye and know what you need to do to take your life to the next level, press through them, and escape the death zone of life. As Jack Canfield quotes so well, "Everything you want in life is on the other side of fear."

Please go to YouTube and listen to the song by Zack Williams, "Fear is a Liar." It will inspire and encourage you greatly as you face your fears.

In the next chapter, we will continue developing a more positive mindset by addressing how you talk to yourself. The words, phrases, and beliefs repeated to yourself have impacted where you are today.

Thinking About My Comfort Zone and Fear

In general, how has fear impacted where you are today in life? What tipping-point decisions have you made in your life that were fear-based?

Have you operated more in the *"death zone"* or the *"faith zone?"* How has living in your comfort zone impacted your career, relationships, finances, and place in life today?

As you look over your top fears, how often has the phrase *"I can't handle it"* been part of those fears?

Think about this for a moment: Your #1 fear is wiped out and no longer exists. Is it not a factor in your life today. Describe in detail how that impacts everything you do, say, think, and believe? How is your life different?

You have the power of the Creator of the Universe inside of you, and He has given you the capability to have all the skills, strengths, and talent you need to succeed. What about your fears makes them bigger than God Himself? What can't you handle?

11

Crushing Your Limiting Beliefs and Learning to Talk Again

"Man often becomes what he believes himself to be. If I keep on saying to myself that I cannot do a certain thing, it is possible that I may end up really becoming incapable of doing it. On the contrary, if I have the belief that I can do it, I shall surely acquire the capacity to do it even if I may not have it at the beginning."
Mahatma Gandi, Indian civil rights movement leader

Then Jesus said to the centurion, "Go your way; and as you have believed, so let it be done for you."
Matthew 8:13 (NKJV)

One of my favorite stories about the power of belief comes from the 1950s. Before May 6, 1954, no one in human history had run the mile in less than four minutes. Most people believed that this was physically impossible. Many so-called experts believed it was beyond the human body's capability to run the mile in under four minutes. Not only that, they went on to say that a person who seriously attempted this feat would end up with lungs that explode and certain death. For many years this belief was perceived as a fact. During this period, a lot of athletes tried to break this barrier without any success.

Sir Roger Gilbert Bannister was a British middle-distance athlete and neurologist. At the 1952 Olympics in Helsinki, Bannister set a British record in the 1500 meters and finished fourth. But on May 6, 1954, Roger Bannister, armed only with the power of belief and incredible determination, ran the mile in 3 minutes and 59 seconds. By doing so, he didn't just create a world record. He also broke a false belief that existed in the minds of thousands of runners that to run a mile in less than four minutes was not possible. And believe it or not, several more people broke the barrier one year later. Today, this is common-place. So what does it mean? It means the barrier never existed at all; it was just a barrier that existed in the minds of men, not in nature! The "impossible was accomplished."

Another tremendous historical moment about the power of belief is the invention of the airplane and the story of two brothers who dared to believe they could make men fly. Their names were Wilbur and Orville Wright. Neither of the Wright brothers had finished high school. They owned a bicycle shop. Imagine what would have happened if they held onto a belief that they were no good since they had very little formal educa-tion? Imagine if they listened to everyone who said man could never fly.

The Wright brothers accomplished the unbelievable because they dared to harness the power of belief and combine it with action. And that's precisely why we will remember them as long as man records history.

What is the takeaway from these two historically gigantic events? The most powerful thing in the world is not a weapon— it is a persistent belief so deeply ingrained in your subconscious mind that it propels every decision you make. People possessed by such intense beliefs can change the world for the better or worse. Because the stronger their beliefs and subsequent actions are, the greater the chances are others will be affected by it and start believing in it. Like in the case of Roger Bannister, the Wright Brothers, and thousands of other examples worldwide.

A *belief* is the state of mind in which a person thinks something to be the case, with or without empirical evidence to prove it with factual certainty. *Limiting beliefs* are something you believe to be true that limits you in some way. These beliefs can be about you, other people, or the world in general. A limiting belief holds you back from making different choices. They keep you from seeing different opportunities. They can also keep you stuck, thinking only about the negative aspects of yourself.

Beliefs come from family, teachers, coaches, media, society, culture, and repeated thoughts that are generally formed during childhood among the people we interact with the most.

Here are some examples of limiting beliefs:

I am not good enough.

I don't deserve this.

I am not enough.

There is not enough for everyone, so I will do the right thing and miss out.

I don't want people to think I am_____.

I don't trust myself.

I can't handle it.

I am going to fail, so why bother trying.

I have to earn the right to be worthy.

I am all wrong; I need to be fixed.

Behavioral research suggests that over 90% of everything we think is an unconscious replay of the already wired programs in our brains. Many of those programs we replay with self-talk are false, damaging programs. And most of them were put there by someone else. The good news is that you can change these patterns.

Self-talk is a way for you to get positive new programs wired into your brain. Your brain records every message you give it. The brain records those messages and doesn't know the difference between something **TRUE** and something **FALSE**. The same goes for positive or negative, bad or good; your brain just records it and then **ACTS** on it. Any message you send to your brain repeatedly (by reading, speaking, or listening) gets wired in, and your brain acts on it as though it is **TRUE**...whether or not it is.

Unfortunately, estimates say **75%** or more of all of the programs each of us has right now are negative, false, counter-productive, or working against us. Negative self-talk tells us that we deserve **LESS** than the best. I believe with all my heart that every person was created and designed to succeed and excel. The reality is that blessings are given in direct proportion to our intention of receiving them, our willingness to work for them, and our willingness to believe in them. You accept and create what you believe you deserve. See why positive self-talk is so critical?

We use self-talk all of the time. Either out loud or to ourselves, we are talking to ourselves. Without really thinking about it, we carry on a running conversation with ourselves and tell ourselves something all the time, and it could be true or false. It could also be positive, or it could be negative. The words you say, especially the words you say when you talk to yourself, not only change your day, they change your life.

What does positive self-talk actually do for you? It helps to paint a new picture of who you're choosing to become. The brain listens best to directions that are specific and detailed. The better your brain can visualize it, the more it works to help you create it. Your brain will work hardest at helping you get those things that you can most clearly imagine.

I remember when I was a teenager and had a severe case of acne on my face and my back. I took medication for it that made my skin dry out, my lips would dry and crack, and my face turned red. Needless to say, when I looked in the mirror every morning, my self-talk was very negative. I would say things like:

- *"Man, you are one ugly dude."*
- *"There is no way any girl would ever be attracted to me."*
- *"Oh my God, that zit on my forehead looks like Mount St. Helens ready to explode."*
- *"My face is so red I look like a tomato."*
- *"You will never amount to anything looking like that."*

No wonder my high school years weren't very memorable or frankly very positive because everything I said about myself was usually negative. I did not realize or understand back then that the thoughts you think and the words you say physically and chemically change your brain, which wires your brain to succeed or fail. All of our self-talk, conscious or unconscious, is helping to wire our brains.

Feeding your brain the right self-talk messages physically rewires your brain over time with positive, new neuropathways that create the new you with better programs. Your daily success depends on the number of positive neuropathways you wire into your brain. Remember when we discussed mindset and referred to *neuroplasticity*- your brain's ability to change and reorganize itself, both physically and functionally continually. The most important rule of neuroplasticity for rewiring the brain is **REPETITION.**

Repetition is the key to rewiring your brain in the right way because of how neuropathways form. Neuropathways are formed in the brain by repeatedly sending electrical and chemical messages (your thoughts) over the same route, like building a highway. Research has shown that positive thinking grows new neurons in the left pre-frontal cortex of your brain and boosts your ability to see alternative solutions. By forming these new connections, you increase the chances of making better choices and becoming more successful.

If you repeat something over and over to yourself, your subconscious mind will eventually begin to accept it as fact. When something has been accepted as truth by your subconscious mind, it will work extra hard to transform the idea into physical reality.

Researchers found that you stop sending fuel to a program's neuropathway when you cease using it. You stop feeding it, and with time, your brain will delete it. In neuroscience it is known as **"pruning."** The brain will get rid of neuropathways you're no longer using to make way for new pathways to form. With enough repetition, the new program, new self-talk will become more potent than the old, negative neuropathway.

When it comes to re-wiring your brain, you have to become aware of what you say to yourself and notice what triggers cause you to say it. You have to choose to get rid of the old and replace it with the new. You have to be intentional and focused, and it needs to be a priority for you in your life. For anything to become a new habit or new neuropathway, put emotion into your new self-talk and visualize the effects on you and your surroundings. Adding emotion and visualization to the practice will help you build those pathways faster and stronger as you repeat the new words or phrases over and over. Finally, you have to believe 100% and be all in with what the truth is about you.

Examples of Positive Self-Talk for You to Practice:

"Today, I am focused. When I have something that needs to be done or accomplished, I practice the success principle of controlled attention. I focus all my energy and attention on one thing at a time. Because I have laser beam focus, I stay on task, I see what needs to be done, and I get it done!"

"It's not what has happened in my past that matters anymore; it's how I move beyond it that counts. It's not about what I have had to endure or been challenged with; it's what I choose to do next that has the potential to create the incredible life I have before me."

"If it's to be, it's up to me. I let nothing or no one take my goals and dreams away from me. I hold the key that opens the door to my unlimited future. I see it, I claim it; the future is mine. What I do with it is up to me."

If you want more information on self-talk, check out the book *What To Say When You Talk To Your Self* by Shad Helmstetter, Ph.D. I also recommend his book *365 Days of Positive Self-Talk*. My wife and I read it together every morning with our devotional.

The next chapter will be crucial in the *Power to Thrive* coaching system. We will focus on where your true power comes from and how to maximize it in your life.

Thinking About My Beliefs and Self-Talk

What are the top three limiting beliefs you have told yourself up to this point in your life? How have they impacted your life outcomes and important decisions?

1.

2.

3.

What is one belief that would change the entire course of your life if you turned it from a negative to a positive? What self-talk do you need to re-program in your brain?

12

The Missing Link to Human Performance and Achievement

"Our world is constantly changing but the needs of our hearts remain the same, and so does God's power to transform our lives and give us hope for the future."
Billy Graham, evangelist, author, and thought leader

"[He was] the true light which gives light to every person coming into the world."
John 1:9 (WE)

odern sports have tried for years to get an extra edge on human performance. The goal was always to endure longer, go faster, throw longer, hit harder, and be stronger. Athletic doping in the 21st century, whether in cycling or any other sport, is part of an athletic enhancement regimen as scientific as nutrition and weight training. It is systematic, both in its programmatic nature and its pervasive reach. In the 1990s and 2000s, these systems may have reached their peaks. There was the fallout with Lance Armstrong and the cycling world with their EPO, HGH, Andriol, and blood transfusion debacle that destroyed the credibility of the Tour de France and cycling in general.

When asked this question by Le Monde, a French magazine, "When you raced, was it possible to perform without doping?" Lance Armstrong responded: "That depends on which races you wanted to win. The Tour de France? No. Impossible to win without doping. Because the Tour is a test of endurance where oxygen is decisive."

And Major League Baseball has also grappled with a doping legacy as well. The record books are full of these players' names, and they all carry a taint of performance-enhancing drugs. The names Bonds, Clemens, Palmeiro, Sosa, A-Rod, Manny, and Big Papi are just a few.

The Russians and their history of Olympic performance enhancement drug usage are unforgettable. Systematic doping in Russian sports has resulted in 47 Olympic medals and dozens of world championships stripped from Russian athletes—the most of any country. Russia's offense rate is more than four times the number of the runner-up and more than 30% of the global total. Russia also has the most athletes caught doping at the Olympic Games, with more than 200. Because of this, in 2019, they were banned from all major sporting events for four years.

Why would these athletes and organizations do this? The answer is quite simple, to enhance human performance to such a degree that winning and raking in millions of dollars is the inevitable outcome. It's about giving yourself an edge, a step up on your fellow competitors. But I believe there is a much better and more substantial way to enhance human performance.

There is a supernatural way to increase human performance better than any steroid, hormone, blood transfusion, or supplement in the marketplace today. I believe that every person is born and created with a spiritual dimension to their life. By tapping into that spiritual power, you increase your performance and positive outcomes by at least **25%**. With this power, you will have an edge. That edge is having the Creator of the universe back you up with power, strength, and might. You'll have the one true God by your side for everything you do.

We all come from different backgrounds and belief systems. But no matter where you come from or what you believe, the one root problem we all have—the #1 factor in our human performance—is this thing called **"SIN."** Our culture has taught us to focus on symptoms, but the root of every problem is always the same thing = **SIN.**

The word Sin is mentioned in the Bible many times. It refers to being an offender or committing an offense against the God of Heaven and His standards. It also means to miss the mark. The word Sin is an archery term. Yes, I mean the full-fledged bow and arrow, Hunger Games, hunting, Olympics event, aimed at the target, hit the bullseye archery. It's nearly impossible to hit the center. That is why this is an excellent illustration of sin. When you miss the bulls-eye center, it is sin because you missed the mark.

Think of it this way, the Creator of the universe and the God we are accountable for our actions to is holy. He cannot be around any sin, and therefore we cannot be in a right relationship with God or go to Heaven if we have sinned (missed the mark). The Bible tells us in Romans 3:23, "For everyone has sinned; we all fall short of God's glorious standard." That means that none of us can tell God, *"I'm a good person, and you should let me go to Heaven."*

Sometimes, we commit sins of omission (we didn't do something that we should have), and sometimes we commit sins of commission (we did something we knew we shouldn't have). Both are off-center, missing the mark. Our best intentions don't qualify us for Heaven. Every one of us has failed to meet God's standard of perfection, which is His Holy Ten Commandments and the truths He has asked us to obey.

All sin separates us from God. Whether you have a slight bitterness, tell a colossal lie that hurts a bunch of people, fail to help someone when you have the opportunity, or living with your boyfriend or girlfriend—by not obeying the Holy Spirit, all of these have **"missed the mark."**

From my personal experience and life, the faith that most effectively deals with this problem is *Christianity*.

Question: If you were in front of God and God asked you, *"Why should I let you into My Heaven?"* What would be your response? Do you know for sure that you are going to heaven? Would you say things like these to explain why you should go to Heaven:

I'm a good and honest person.

I was raised in the church.

I believe in God.

I tithe faithfully.

I am a Catholic, Baptist, Methodist, Adventist, Mormon, Presbyterian, Lutheran, Protestant, etc.

My heart is for helping others.

I read the Bible, pray, and go to church.

I got baptized.

I love everyone, and I am not racist.

My entire family is Christian.

I act appropriately—friendly to others, and I am not rude to people.

If your answers are listed above, you should be concerned because none of those things in and of themselves will get you into Heaven.

Take a good look at your life and simply acknowledge that sin is what is keeping you from a life of total success. Then write down what sins you think hold you back. Include the symptoms they bring about in your life. Many of these symptoms are internal, like anger, guilt, shame, lack of meaning and purpose, lack of self-worth, etc.

The good news for you today is that the answer is straightforward and laid out in Acts 4:12, where it says, "Nor is there salvation in any other, for there is no other name under heaven given among men by which we must be saved."

Your Personal Road to Salvation Through God's Words

1. The Human Problem (Romans 5:12). The first and most important truth in your salvation is to realize that you are sinful. Everyone who has existed since Adam and Eve in the Garden of Eden is a sinner. That is why death exists in this world today.

"As it is written: 'There is no one righteous, not even one.'" (Romans 3:10)

"For all have sinned and fall short of the glory of God." (Romans 3:23)

2. After establishing that "all have sinned," Romans 6:23 explains the depth of this problem and its consequences.

"For the wages of sin is death…" (Romans 6:23)

However, the second half of the verse should give you hope as a sinner that you can experience eternal life and salvation through Jesus Christ.

"…but the gift of God is eternal life in Christ Jesus our Lord." (Romans 6:23)

3. Humanity's Hope in Christ (Romans 5:8). Because God is love, even though you are a sinner, He further explains the hope we have in the love of God expressed through Christ.

"But God demonstrates His own love for us in this: While we were still sinners, Christ died for us." (Romans 5:8)

4. God's love for you is so great He willingly gave up His only Son, Jesus Christ, for you that when you believe in Him, you may have everlasting life. (John 3:16-17) The good news in all this is that there is no condemnation from God towards you at all. He loves you and wants you to be saved through His Son, Jesus Christ.

"For God so loved the world that He gave His only begotten Son, that whoever believes in Him should not perish but have everlasting life. For God did not send His Son into the world to condemn the world, but that the world through Him might be saved."

5. How does God forgive you of your Sin? (1 John 1:9) By now, you should understand your condition, how much God loves you, and that He would provide a solution to your sin problem. It's time for you to follow through with the prescription for your illness. To do so, you need to tell the Lord God Almighty your sins and then believe He has forgiven you completely.

"If we confess our sins, He is faithful and just to forgive us our sins and to cleanse us from all unrighteousness."

6. Once you confess your sins and are forgiven then comes the part many have a challenge with, turning the other direction and moving away from sin in your life. The Bible refers to this as **"repentance"**.

Acts 3:19, "Repent therefore and be converted, that your sins may be blotted out, so that the times of refreshing may come from the presence of the Lord."

7. If you by faith believe in your heart and openly speak it, that Jesus Christ is your Lord and Savior and that His Heavenly Father raised Him from the dead, then the Bible says under no uncertain terms, You will be saved!

"If you declare with your mouth, 'Jesus is Lord,' and believe in your heart that God raised Him from the dead, you will be saved. For it is with your heart that you believe and are justified, and it is with your mouth that you profess your faith and are saved." (Romans 10:9-10)

"For, 'Everyone who calls on the name of the Lord will be saved.'" (Romans 10:13)

"Therefore, since we have been justified through faith, we have peace with God through our Lord Jesus Christ, through whom we have gained access by faith into this grace in which we now stand." (Romans 5:1-2)

Romans 8:1 rejoices in the result of salvation. Before faith in Christ, all who have sinned were condemned by their sin and destined for death. But now, with faith in Christ, "there is no condemnation," and believers are gifted eternal life with God.

8. Put your past and former life behind you. One of the great blessings you receive when you give your life to Jesus Christ is to wipe your slate clean. You get a 'do-over.' You receive a second chance to live your life according to God's purpose and plan for you. All your mistakes, bad decisions, disobedience, ungodly living, everything contrary to God is forgiven, wiped clean, and is no longer a part of your life in God's eyes. There still may be consequences to your sins, and God will help you see your way through all that. This is what being **Born Again** is all about.

2 Corinthians 5:17, "Therefore, if anyone is in Christ, he is a new creation; old things have passed away; behold all things have become new."

Jesus Christ tells us Himself in John 3:5-8 that you must be born again to enter the Kingdom of God. He desires to give you a new heart, new mind, new habits, and a new way of life. It's like you are starting life all over again. Everything is fresh, new, and seen from a Godly and spirit perspective.

"Unless one is born of water and the Spirit, he cannot enter the kingdom of God. That which is born of the flesh is flesh, and that which is born of the Spirit is spirit. Do not marvel that I said to you, You must be born again."

9. The best news of all, you can now know for sure that by God's grace, you are saved by faith in Jesus Christ. It's not about what you do or don't do, although living for Jesus means walking in

newness of life and not doing the things the world engages in that will take you off track, its knowing that if you have Jesus Christ, you have everything.

1 John 5:11-13, "And this is the record: that God has given us eternal life, and this life is in His Son. He who has the Son has life; he who does not have the Son of God does not have life. These things I have written to you who believe in the name of the Son of God, that you may know that you have eternal life, and that you may continue to believe in the name of the Son of God."

10. Because of your great love for the Lord, live each day for Him. With the remaining days of your life, know that you are new and born again. Obedience to His word and commands becomes a daily part of your life and enduring in your faith. Never let go of Jesus Christ; stay connected and thriving in Him till the day you breathe your last breath.

1 Peter 1:13-15, "So prepare your minds for service and have self-control. All your hope should be for the gift of grace that will be yours when Jesus Christ is shown to you. Now that you are obedient children of God do not live as you did in the past… But be holy in all you do, just as God, the one who called you, is holy."

1 Corinthians 15:1-2, "Now brothers and sisters, I want you to remember the Gospel I preached to you, which you received and in which you stand strong, by which also you are saved, if you continue believing the word I preached to you, unless you believed in vain."

If you have walked yourself through the above pathway for salvation through Jesus Christ, now pray this prayer between you and the Lord and believe you are new and saved through the sacrifice and love God has for you in His Son, Jesus Christ:

"Dear God, because I am a sinner, I accept Jesus Christ as my Lord and Savior for my life, and I accept that there is only one way to have my sins forgiven and to gain entrance into heaven for

eternity, and that is the through the saving grace and sacrificial blood of the Son of God who is Jesus Christ. I desire to repent and turn from my old way of life and be born again into God's love, His grace, His ways, and I look forward to living my life in accordance with the Bible."

The next step for you is to find a Bible-believing church. A place where you can grow, thrive, and prosper under the training and influence of the Holy Spirit and receive teaching that will help you grow and mature in your walk with God and then make your public commitment to be baptized and express your love and belief in Jesus.

Do you know why it's important how you live your earthly life? It matters because you set the stage for eternity with it. This life for you may only be for a short time, or maybe well into your late 80s or 90s, but the great news is that eternity with the Lord is never-ending and everlasting. How you live right now is creating your resume for eternity.

Are you using your God-given gifts and talents to bring glory to Him or yourself?

Are you truly living up to the ideals and standards that God has for you written in His Word?

Is your life a reflection of the things of this world, or are you reflecting God's character to others?

Evidence of Salvation in Jesus Christ

You will have 100% faith in Jesus Christ as your savior and His saving power alone.

You will have a greater sense of your sinfulness more and more, and you will see your great need for a Savior.

You will admit that God's laws and ways are the best for you to thrive in this life.

You will confess your sins and grow in repentance.

You will be a new creation, not living in the past. Love will begin to be the foundation of your life and relationships.

Daily desire to read the Bible and spend time with the Lord through prayer and meditation. A book that I recommend that changed my paradigm on this subject is called, "2 Chairs" written by Bob Beaudine. Visit www.BobBeaudine.com Spending time with God activates hope, optimism, creativity, and the plan.

You will have new desires and a stronger affection for Christ and dependence on Him.

God will work in your life to make you into the image of His Son.

You will desire to have fellowship with Christ daily and weekly and with other Christians.

You will grow and produce fruit by being a faithful witness and ambassador for Jesus.

You will feel an inner drive and passion to serve the Lord with your spiritual gifts and living out His purpose in your life.

Here is the GREAT news because in JESUS CHRIST...

I Am Accepted
John 1:12 I am God's child.
John 15:15 I am Christ's friend.
Rom. 5:1 I have been justified.

1 Cor. 6:17 I am united with the Lord, and I am one spirit with Him.

1 Cor. 6:19-20 I have been bought with a price. I belong to God.

1 Cor. 12:27 I am a member of Christ's body.

Eph. 1:5 I have been adopted as God's child.

Eph. 2:18 I have direct access to God through the Holy Spirit.

Col. 1:14 I have been redeemed and forgiven of all my sins.

Col. 2:10 I am complete in Christ.

John 5:24 I stand tall under no condemnation.

I Am Secure

Jude 1:24 I am faultless before God.

Rom. 8:28 I am assured that all things work together for good.

Rom. 8:1-2, 31-34 I am free from any condemning charges against me.

Rom. 8:35-39 I cannot be separated from the love of God.

Phil. 1:6 I am confident that the good work that God has begun in me will be perfected.

2 Tim. 1:7 I have not been given a spirit of fear but of power, love, and a sound mind.

Heb. 4:16 I can find grace and mercy to help in time of need.

1 Cor. 15:57 I have victory in Christ now.

I Am Significant

Matt. 5:13-14 I am the salt and light of the earth.

John 15:1-5 I am a branch of the true Vine, a channel of His life.

John 15:16 I have been chosen and appointed to bear fruit.

Acts 1:8 I am a personal witness of Christ.

2 Cor. 5:17-21 I am a minister of reconciliation for God.

2 Cor. 6:1 I am God's coworker (1 Cor. 3:9).

Eph. 2:10 I am God's workmanship.

Eph. 3:12 I may approach God with freedom and confidence.

Phil. 4:13 I can do all things through Christ who strengthens me.

God's Love Letter to You

To My Priceless Beloved Child,

Today you discovered more about your divine design. When I planted these gifts into the treasure place of your heart, I knew one day that you would seek them out and use them to fulfill your purpose. Today is that day.

You were born with gifts, talents, and abilities. The day I created you and formed you in your mother's womb was a day I will never forget. I made you unique and poured my favor upon you. I have watched you grow, and I have walked by your side every step of the way.

Right now, it is your responsibility to discover everything you can about the reason and purpose for your existence and then convey that to others. My vision may not be what everyone else has in mind or even what you may see as your vision for your life. When you truly understand the reason for your existence, I promise you personal fulfillment, satisfaction, and peace of mind that My purpose for your life will be in you. Search for it with your entire heart and mind, seek your God-given purpose and utilize it for the betterment of humanity. Tap into my infinite wisdom and understanding, and allow me to help you pull out My purpose from your heart.

My child, I gave you a unique identity and purpose for your life. I designed for you a specific role to fulfill. Live out that role because your destiny awaits you. I am always here for you, and I will never leave you neither forsake you. You are mine, important, unique, and priceless beyond measure. Just know always and never forget:

Your life has a purpose…
Your story is important…
Your dreams count…
Your voice matters…
You were born to make an impact!
My love is with you always and forever,

Your Heavenly Father, Creator,

and Master of the Universe, I AM

If you are looking for true liberation in your life and walking closer with God than you ever have before, then Chapter 13 is going to change your life forever. Here is where you begin to walk, talk, and live in the power of the Lord Jesus Christ.

Thinking About High Performance and Achievement in My Relationship with God

What **limiting beliefs** keep you from fully embracing the Christian faith?

What impact has Sin had on your life? How has it impacted your thoughts, words, actions, habits, and character?

Your favorite scriptures tend to become the script or pattern for your life...the promises of God become the storyline of your life. The more you rehearse these scriptures, the more you start living them out. They become your thoughts and desires. Write down your top five scriptures from the Bible and contemplate how they have impacted your life.

1.

2.

3.

4.

5.

Read through God's Love Letter to you several times. What jumps out at you that stirs your heart? What are some concepts you can employ in your everyday living?

PART THREE

Physical and Mental Health Will Lead to Emotional Well-Being

"If you want to be happy, set a goal that commands your thoughts, liberates your energy, and inspires your hopes."
Andrew Carnegie, richest man in the world in the early 1900s

"Beloved, I pray that you may prosper in all things and be in health, just as your soul prospers."
3 John 2 (NKJV)

13

Living in the Rear- View Mirror of Life and the "F" Word

*"Resentment is like drinking poison and then hop-
ing it will kill your enemies."*
Nelson Mandela, winner of the Nobel Peace Prize

"Then Peter came to Him and said, 'Lord, how often
shall my brother sin against me, and I forgive him? Up
to seven times?' Jesus said to him, 'I do not say to you,
up to seven times, but up to seventy times seven.'"
Matthew 18: 21-22 (NKJV)

If the best part of your life is **in the past**, then something is
terribly wrong. As we get older, we are supposed to be **more**
competent, not less. Life is supposed to get **better** because we
are supposed to be **better** at it. Many people live in the rear-view

mirror of life—living in the past and allowing that to dictate their future, direction, and outcomes in life. This mindset creates a significant challenge to overcome for them.

The truth is, you need to let go of the past so you can embrace the future.

One of the most moving stories about forgiveness is the story of Renee Napier and Eric Smallridge. Their story has touched millions of lives to date, and I hope it will stir something in you today.

One of the top Christian songs of 2012, "Forgiveness," written by Matthew West, was inspired by a mother dealing with her daughter's death at the hands of a drunk driver. The song is about Renee Napier, who lost her daughter, Megan, in a car accident at the hands of a drunk driver, a 24-year-old named Eric Smallridge, a great young man by all accounts but made a tragic mistake. Renee's been on a journey of hatred and bitterness, and she's learned how to forgive the young man who took her beloved daughter's life.

After Megan died in 2001, Renee began speaking and giving presentations. In time, God put it on her heart to forgive this man miraculously and reach out to him in prison. Until she was free of the anger and bitterness that she held towards Eric, she would be the prisoner even though he was the one behind bars.

As a result of Renee, Eric surrendered his life to Jesus Christ as his Lord and Savior. They developed a unique friendship—she feels like she gained a son and even went before the court to cut Eric's sentence in half. He made a terrible mistake taking the life of two young girls, and yet he's forgiven. Renee told him that she serves a God who commands her to forgive, and she needed to be set free as much for herself as for him. Eric left prison in November of 2012, and he's standing by Renee's side as they travel the country, speaking together to young people about the dangers of drinking and driving and the power of forgiveness. Renee's story is life-defining, and we all need to think about how forgiveness can set us free.

Take a moment to pause here and write down the top three most significant times in your life when you felt victimized, mistreated, or dealt with unfairly. Write enough detail to capture the emotion if you can. Remember and bring to life the incident, including the people involved and the emotions you feel.

Now write down how each of those times impacted your life—your ambition, courage, fears, what you didn't receive, what was taken from you, what part you might have to accept responsibility for, etc.

As you wrote them, I am guessing you felt some emotions all over again you thought were behind you. You are still being affected by something that occurred in your past, affecting some of your outcomes today. The reality is that anger, bitterness, resentment, and the desire for revenge can waste valuable energy. Energy depleted from positive, goal-directed action.

The Law of Attraction is a universal law of the mind that says you attract more of whatever feelings you are experiencing. Being angry, hostile, and unforgiving about a past hurt only ensures that you will attract more of the same into your life.

So what is the anecdote for anger, bitterness, resentment?

What can you do today to make painful and hurtful things of your past take their rightful place in the rear-view mirror of your life?

The answer is plain and simple: Forgiveness.
When you forgive, it puts you back in the present—where good things can happen to you and where you can take action to create future gains for yourself, your team, your company, and your family. Staying stuck in the muck and mire of the past uses valuable energy and robs you of the personal power you need to forge ahead and create what you want.

What hurts you the most now is harboring anger, resentment, bitterness towards others and replaying the same hatred over and over again in your mind. The word *forgive* really means to give it up for yourself and not for them.

In the bestselling book and popular movie, *The Shack*, author William P. Young paints a beautiful picture of God explaining the process of forgiveness to Mack, the main character in the book whose little girl was murdered:

Mack: "How can I ever forgive that man who killed my Missy? I want him to hurt like he hurt me...if I can't get justice, I still want revenge."

God: "Mack, for you to forgive this man is for you to release him to me and allow me to redeem him."

Mack: "Redeem him? ... I don't want you to redeem him! I want you to hurt him, to punish him, to put him in hell... I just can't forget what he did, can I?"

God: "Forgiveness is not about forgetting, Mack. It is about letting go of another person's throat."

Mack: "So what then? I just forgive him and everything is okay, and we become buddies?"

God: "You don't have a relationship with this man, at least not yet. Forgiveness does not establish a relationship."

God: "Forgiveness is first for you, the forgiver ... to release you from something that will eat you alive; that will destroy your joy and your ability to love fully and openly."

I also like this quote from award-winning author Isabelle Holland, "As long as you don't forgive, who and whatever is it will occupy rent-free space in your mind."

Common Questions and Misconceptions about Forgiveness:

Who is forgiveness for, the offender or the offended? Forgiveness is for you; it's for the offended. It releases you from the emotional control of another.

If you don't forgive, are you empowering them? Absolutely; they have control over you emotionally.

If I forgive someone, am I letting them off the hook or not be accountable? It is not about them at all; it's about your freedom. There are always consequences for our actions. The offender will have to pay the price for that eventually, in this world or the next.

If I forgive my offender, does that mean I have to forget what happened to me? The brain is wired not to allow you to do that. Your experiences in life are all stored in your subconscious mind. By forgiving, you will be able to have peace and eliminate the emotional control of another. Your experience is part of your history; it happened and cannot be rewritten. But by forgiving, you will think about it less and less every day. You'll be able to move on with your life and not be in the pain, hurt, and offense so much. Maybe even use your story to help others.

What if I am not ready to meet them face to face to forgive them? Most of the time, it's **NOT** a good idea to meet with them. Defense mechanisms will be up, and it would likely be awkward at best. Denial would more than likely rule the day. You can forgive someone or something without having them in front of you. Forgiveness is about you being free. It's releasing their emotional control over you.

Forgiveness is simply breaking the **emotional bond** tied to the person or circumstances that offended you. It's about not being held hostage anymore. **Freedom** is what you do with what's been done to you. You have a choice because forgiveness is for you, so you can **be free** to move on.

Forgiveness is about doing whatever it takes to preserve the power to create your emotional state. It's about being able to say, *"You cannot hurt me and then control me, even in your absence, by turning my heart cold and changing who I am and what I value. I make these choices about how I feel and how I live; I will not give you the power."*

For some of you, this might be the most powerful chapter in this book. I will tell you, if you are harboring anger, resentment, and bitterness towards something or someone, then everything we have covered up to this point will be challenging for you to implement because of the negative impact unforgiveness has on you. When you release the poison, the evil, the negative stronghold from inside you, it's like a butterfly appearing from a cocoon, transformed! It's beautiful, and different, and it begins a new chapter and stage in its life. That's what happens to you when you forgive and let go of those things holding you back.

Philippians 3:13-14: "Brothers, I do not consider that I have made it my own. But one thing I do: forgetting what lies behind and straining forward to what lies ahead, I press on toward the goal for the prize of the upward call of God in Christ Jesus."

Mark 11:25: "And whenever you stand praying, forgive, if you have anything against anyone, so that your Father also who is in heaven may forgive you your trespasses."

Colossians 3:12-13: "Clothe yourselves with compassion, kindness, humility, gentleness and patience. Bear with each other and forgive one another if any of you has a grievance against someone. Forgive as the Lord forgave you."

I have outlined below how to practice and implement the act and habit of forgiveness. Once you learn this and begin to act on it daily, it will be as you have been born again, which in reality, you have. You can do this by yourself but make sure you are in front of a mirror. It can simulate in a way as if you are talking to someone else. I recommend if you do this with your spouse, partner, counselor, or therapist, that you sit across from them and hold their hands for emotional support. This is not about having a conversation with another person; it's about getting out the pain, anger, sadness, and grief inside of you.

Step 1, write down the name(s) of the people or institutions that you need to forgive to have emotional, physical, and mental peace in your life. Then pick the one that is causing you the most pain in your life right now, which has the most prominent negative influence upon your life. The one that, if released from inside of you, would give you the most peace.

Step 2, write down how anger, bitterness, resentment, frustration, and revenge impact your physical health right now. How do you feel physically and emotionally? How is it impacting your relationships? Your work?

Step 3, go through the road to forgiveness below. Take your time and flush it out thoroughly.

The Road to Forgiveness

1. Identify the offender and the offense. Say it out loud.

2. Recreate the pain by acknowledging your pain, anger, resentment about the situation.

3. Acknowledge the fears and self-doubts that it created for you in your life.

4. Acknowledge what you wanted and didn't get and what was taken from you.

5. Accept any responsibility you played in letting it occur or continue.

6. Choose and decide to forgive. Say out loud, **"I am ready to be FREE!"**

7. Say the names of the offenses in detail, then say the words, **"I forgive you for _____."**

8. Let go and forgive. Say the words **"I forgive you"** multiple times.

9. May need to forgive them every day, multiples times a day, to release their control over you

Forgiveness Self-Talk for you: *I release myself from all the inner poison of unforgiveness that has kept me limited, and I now allow myself to be free. I forgive myself, and I forgive others. I am free. I know that I deserve what God has and wants for me, and I release all expectations and demands I have placed on others. I choose to be free today.*

14

Building Margin into Your Life to Lower Your Stress

"I believe that the greatest gift you can give your family and the world is a healthy you."
Joyce Meyer, author, speaker, ministry leader

"The key question to keep asking is, 'Are you spending your time on the right things?' Because time is all you have."
Randy Pausch, American Professor of Computer Science & cancer victim

Matthew 6:23-34: Do not worry or be anxious for tomorrow, live in the present today.

"Haven't you yet learned that your body is the home of the Holy Spirit God gave you, and that He lives

within you...so use every part of your body to give
glory back to God, because He owns it."
1 Corinthians 6:19-20 (TLB)

There is a synergistic relationship between the mind and the body, for they are one. Whatever has a negative effect on the mind will have a negative effect on the body. The reverse is true as well. *To neglect the body is to neglect the mind.*

Stress and anxiety are strong influencers with sickness and disease in the human body. Americans are the most stressed people globally; between 75-90% of all visits to the doctor are due to stress-related disorders.

Ignoring who you honestly and authentically are, can be the making of your physical, mental, and emotional downfall. If you ignore who you are, your bodily system could be so distressed that it will wear out, and you will be old beyond your years. Forcing yourself to be someone you are not, or stuffing down who you are, stresses and taxes the mind, body, and soul. It will shorten your life span and the quality of your life.

A change in your mental attitude as well will help the development of bodily resistance against sickness and disease.

Sickness of the mind is prevalent everywhere. A large percent of the diseases from which people suffer have their foundation here! There is an intimate connection between the mind and the body, and what affects one impacts the other -The brain is the organ and instrument of the mind and controls the whole body. Today, stress is one of the most significant causes of physical symptoms, including headaches, upset stomach, elevated blood pressure, chest pain, heart problems, diabetes, skin conditions, asthma, arthritis, depression, anxiety, and sleeping problems.

According to a recent American Psychiatric Association poll safety, health, and finances seem to be the greatest sources of anxiety. Sixty-eight percent of respondents said *"keeping myself or my family safe" and "my health"* made them either somewhat or extremely anxious. Sixty-seven percent said the same about *"paying my bills or expenses."* Politics and interpersonal relationships followed at 56% and 48%, respectively. Other findings included:

- Forty-three percent of all adults suffer adverse health effects from stress.

- Seventy-five percent to 90% of all doctor's office visits are for stress-related ailments and complaints.

- The Occupational Safety and Health Administration (OSHA) declared stress a hazard of the workplace. Stress costs American industry more than $300 billion annually.

There are four categories of stress: Physical, Emotional, Mental, and Chemical.

Physical Stress has to do with lack of sleep, overworking, excessive exercise, injuries, surgery, infections, disease, and pain.

Emotional Stress or psychological stress is about dealing with and managing anger, hostility, depression, anxiety, fear, and guilt.

Mental Stress has to do with worry and anxiety over debt, overwork, not enough playtime, marriage issues, family issues, feeling overwhelmed, losing control, and feeling trapped in your life.

Chemical Stress has to do with the things we put into our bodies, such as excessive sugar, caffeine, stimulants, alcohol, nicotine, food additives, allergens, pesticides, and pollution.

Your perceptions determine what you label as stressful or not stressful. Stress is largely a matter of what you think about external stimuli and how you respond to them. But let's be honest, since the year 2000, progress has come so fast and the result of that is more and more comes at us faster and faster. Progress tends to flow in the direction of increased pressure and stress that tax our human limits. With the dawn of the personal computer and technology changing back in the 1980s, the promise was that life would get easier. We would have more time, and we would enjoy the things that are important in life. **Has that happened for any of us?**

Think about it. The speed of travel, the power of computers, information, complexity, mobility, speed of communication, the technology explosion, dangers in our world, terrorism, media pervasiveness, media power, specialization, personal and national indebtedness, inflation, cost of goods and services, traffic congestion on land and in air, the prevalence of divorce, daycare for children, racial tensions, political divisiveness, the social media explosion, our education system today, drug addiction issues, our shrinking world, an aging population, and of course sickness, disease, pandemics... all of it impacts us and causes stress levels to skyrocket.

One of my favorite books of all time, written by Dr. Richard Swenson, is called *Margin*. In it, Dr. Swenson describes how we live overloaded lives and that the margin, which is the space that once existed between ourselves and our limits, it's the amount allowed beyond that which is needed. Margin is the gap between rest and exhaustion, the space between breathing freely and suffocating. Margin is the opposite of overload.

Another great point Dr. Swenson mentions in *Margin,* which will lead us into the importance of time and energy management, is the concept of **Power – Load = Margin.**

We have **"power"** when we have energy, skills, time, training, emotional and physical strength, faith, finances, and social support.

Our **"load"** is work, problems, obligations, commitments, expectations, debt, deadlines, and relationship conflicts.

The formula is common sense when you think about it. When your load is greater than your power, you enter into a negative margin, and you become overloaded. When your power is greater than your load, you have margin built into your life. Our challenge is to figure out ways to improve our power and decrease our load so we can operate at the *Power to Thrive* as much as possible. When we hit that goal, we experience emotional and physical energy at the highest levels possible.

The good news is you can learn to manage stress and lead a happier, healthier life.

Here are 11 proven suggestions to help you keep stress at bay:

1. Keep a positive attitude. Mindset is everything, and keeping negativity and pessimism at bay will significantly help keep stress and overload to a minimum.

2. Accept that there are events that you cannot control. This one is so huge. See the diagram below to illustrate this point. This concept changed my life when I read Stephen Covey's best-selling book, *The 7 Habits of Highly Effective People*. The basic premise is to put your focus and energy on things that you can control. Still, there are hundreds of others things that are entirely out of your control. One of the biggest reasons our stress levels rise and margins get minimized is we spend so much time thinking and worrying about these things outside of our control. Doing so significantly increases our stress and anxiety levels. How much time you spend watching TV and online also has a massive influence on where you focus. To thrive in your life, focus on your circle of control, your sphere of influence, and not your circle of concern.

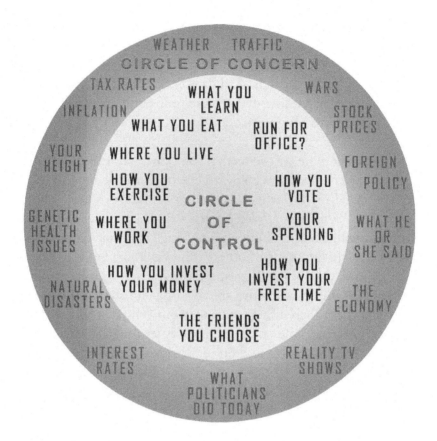

Take a moment and ask yourself how much time are spending in the Circle of Concern? _____%

What areas are you wasting time?

Focus on what you can control, and don't waste energy and time on what you can't!

3. Be emotionally in control by being assertive instead of aggressive. Assert your feelings, opinions, or beliefs instead of becoming angry, defensive, or passive.

4. Learn and practice relaxation techniques; get out in nature, deep breathing, meditation, and stretching.

5. Exercise regularly. Your body can fight stress better when it is fit. Not to mention expending all that energy for 30-40 minutes is a great way to blow out negativity and allow in positivity. Getting fresh air, sunshine, and deep breathing is an excellent recipe for building margin and lowering anxiety in your life.

6. Eat healthy, well-balanced meals. Don't rely on alcohol, drugs, or compulsive behaviors to reduce stress.

7. Make time for hobbies, interests, and relaxation. Find positive ways to release stress and anxiety while incorporating movement.

8. Get enough rest and sleep. Your body needs time to recover from stressful events.

9. Seek out social support. Spend time with family, friends and those who build you up and encourage you.

10. Seek treatment with a psychologist or other mental health professional trained in stress management or biofeedback techniques to learn healthy ways of dealing with the stress in your life. My recommendation is to spend time with the Lord daily in reading the Bible and in prayer. Like Jesus Christ says Himself in Matthew 11:29, "Take my yoke upon you, and learn from me, for I am gentle and lowly in heart, and you will find rest for your souls. For my yoke is easy, and my burden is light."

11. The last area to help you is time management. Focus on the things you value the most, the activities that bring you the highest return on emotional and personal investment. I like what the Bible says in Ephesians 5:15-17, "Look carefully then how you walk, not as unwise but as wise, making the best use of the time, because the days are evil. Don't be foolish, but understand what the will of the Lord is."

Organize and execute around your priorities in life. Time management is kind of a misnomer of sorts; the challenge is really not about managing our time, but managing ourselves. The cold, hard truth is that the way you spend your time results from how much you value your time and what your priorities are! There are two powerful concepts I want to share with you to help manage your time and priorities.

Each of us has only 24 hours on any given day. On average, we spend about nine hours working and seven hours sleeping. This leaves us with eight hours of leftover time, or what we commonly call our "spare" time. But these precious eight hours are really where you see what a person's priorities are, what they value, and how they manage or mismanage their time. Here is my recommendation on the time allotment for how to effectively use those remaining and important eight hours of your life:

1) Spend your first 60 minutes after you awake with these things:

   a) Drink 30 oz of water at a minimum

   b) Gratitude time, personal prayer, scripture affirmations (10 min)

   c) Go over your vision, mission, purpose statements (5 min)

   d) Read through values, roles, goals, positive self-talk (5 min)

   e) Personal devotional or Bible study time (30 min)

   f) Look over your vision board (5 min)

   g) Read over your 60 second commercial about you (5 min)

2) Spend 1 hour getting fresh air, exercise, moving your body, lots of deep breathing

3) Read, study, or watch a video for 30 minutes on personal development, improving yourself

4) Take 30 minutes to reach out by phone, text, email, in person, family members & friends

5) Take 1 hour to do something positive for your community, network, spouse, family

6) Take 2 hours to catch up on your news, sports, weather, TV, social media

7) Spend 3 hours on relaxation, meditation, recreation, responsibilities, music, etc.

Follow this schedule six days per week, and set aside one day per week for nothing but mental, physical, spiritual rejuvenation, and relaxation. On this day of rest, take time for restoring and building up relationships, church related activities, and spending time in nature. Put aside all electronics and communication devices. Give your mind, body, and spirit a chance to relax and reload for another busy week coming up.

The next concept helped lower my stress levels. It also helped me to stop trying to multi-task all the time. It's referred to as the **time chunking method.** This time management method is about two things: working more productively and giving yourself time to rest so your creative juices can flow to the max! Imagine the following being part of your life:

* Being more at peace during your day and cutting your stress levels way down

* Being able to sleep better with less stress

* Maximizing your return on investment, ROI, by working fewer hours per day without negatively impacting your income

* Have more time to spend with family and doing the things you enjoy the most

* Be more focused and get more done with better clarity and creativity

The basic premise of time chunking is that you work for so long and then take a break. This system's design helps you focus on **one** thing for a specific time.

Time chunking limits the amount of time the brain has to focus. Doing so eliminates procrastination. Your attention is focused on one project versus multitasking. This focus method improves task completion.

Here's how it works for me, the variation is flexible and can be different for everyone. I typically work for 60 minutes, then take a ten- minute break. I do this from 8:00 A.M. to 6:00 P.M.

Work for 60 minutes....take a 10 minute break

What makes this work so well? The brain is designed this way. It likes to work in short, focused periods. Once you reach the end of that period, productivity drops dramatically. The great thing about this is you can be flexible with it. You can change the amount of time for both the work period and breaks. Make it unique to you. The idea here is to work a period of time then take a break.

The next chapter is about setting goals and how to focus your mind on what it is that you want in your life. You will put an action plan together for your life.

Thinking About Stress in My Life and Managing My Time

How much does technology rule your life? Are you on call and tied to your phone 24/7?

What are some things you can do to build more margin into your life?

Which of the four stressors are you most prone to Physical, Mental, Emotional, Chemical?

What's one thing you can do today to better manage your time and be more focused on the most important things to you?

15

The Fuel of Life and the Power of Manifesting

"If you want to be happy, set a goal that commands your thoughts, liberates your energy, and inspires your hopes."
Andrew Carnegie, the richest man in
the world in the early 1900s

"A man's heart plans his way, but the Lord directs his steps."
Proverbs 16:9 (NKJV)

I still remember hearing about a docu-movie called *Free Solo* while watching the Academy Awards with my wife, Libia, on February 24, 2019. I immediately went to the internet, downloaded it, and watched it. Wow, a life-changing experience for me. The movie portrays a man who free-soloed El Capitan in Yosemite National Park in California on June 3, 2017. Free soloing is when a climber is alone and uses no ropes or any other equipment to aid or protect him as he climbs. The New York Times described it as "one of the greatest athletic feats of any kind, ever," and I couldn't agree more!

The man who did this impressive feat was renowned rock climber Alex Honnold. Honnold became the first person to scale the iconic nearly 3,000-foot vertical granite wall known as El Capitan without using ropes or other safety gear, completing what may be the most remarkable feat of pure rock climbing in the sport's history.

A team of filmmakers, led by Alex longtime climbing partners Jimmy Chin, and Elizabeth Chai Vasarhelyi, captured the ascent for National Geographic Documentary Films, quite an accomplishment in itself.

What's truly amazing is that Alex had been thinking about what it would take to free solo El Capitan and visualizing this project for years. For more than a year, Honnold trained for the climb at locations in the United States, China, Europe, and Morocco.

What jumps out when you watch this movie is two significant things that Alex did to help him achieve this free solo climb. First, he was obsessed—he was fixated—on his goal of climbing this rock wall. He visualized and mentally played out the climb in his mind daily. He massively prepared for this one-day event that would change his life forever. Second, he learned to dance with fear and press through it.

Some of his poise is from his detailed preparation. He is obsessive about his training, which includes hour-long sessions every other day hanging by his fingertips and doing one- and two-armed pullups on a specially-made apparatus that he bolted into the doorway of his van. He also spends hours perfecting, rehearsing, and memorizing exact sequences of hand and foot placements for every key pitch. He is an obsessive note-taker, logging his workouts and evaluating his performance on every climb in a detailed journal.

"Years ago, when I first mentally mapped out what it would mean to free solo Freerider, there were half a dozen pitches where I was like, 'Oh that's a scary move and that's a really scary sequence, and that little slab, and that traverse,'" Honnold said. "There were so many little sections where I thought 'Ughh—cringe.' But in the years since, I've pushed my comfort zone and made it bigger and bigger until these objectives that seemed totally crazy eventually fell within the realm of the possible."

There are other climbers in Honnold's league physically, but no one else has matched his mental ability to control fear. His tolerance for scary situations is beyond remarkable. Honnold sees it in more pragmatic terms. "With free-soloing, obviously I know that I'm in danger, but feeling fearful while I'm up there is not helping me in any way," he said. "It's only hindering my performance, so I just set it aside and leave it be."

Many people like Alex Hannold, who accomplish incredible things in their lives, live by **three simple rules in life:**

1. If you do not go after what you want, you will never have it

2. If you do not ask, the answer will always be no

3. If you do not step forward, you will always be in the same place

The Bible reflects those rules.

In Matthew 7:7-8 says, "Ask, and it shall be given you; seek, and ye shall find; knock, and it shall be opened unto you: For every one that asks receives; and he that seeks shall find; and to him that knocks the door will be opened."

In Mark 11: 22-24, we read, "And Jesus answered them, "Have faith in God. Truly, I say to you, whoever says to this mountain, 'Be taken up and thrown into the sea,' and does not doubt in his heart, but believes that what he says will come to pass, it will be done for him. Whatever you ask in prayer, believe that you have received it, and it will be yours."

And in 2 Corinthians 5:7, "For we walk by faith, not by sight."

To make sure your plans sync up with what God's plans are for your life, here are some basic questions to ask yourself as you pray and meditate on God's will and direction for your life, and especially as you think about your goals and the things you desire to achieve:

What did you have in mind when You created me?

What do You want to do in and through my life?

How are You working through circumstances I am currently experiencing to prepare me for Your mission in my life?

Is there anyone You want me to minister to or anywhere You desire me to go to represent Your name?

Are my desires and dreams congruent with Your plan for my life?

In Proverbs 16:9, Solomon says, "A man's heart plans his way, But the LORD directs his steps."

Terry Orlick, in his book *In Pursuit of Excellence,* says this about goals, "achieving success and high achievement will be largely dependent upon how well you know where you want to go, how much you want to get there, and the extent to which you believe in your ability to arrive at your desired destination."

Those are the three key points we discussed. You've got to know where you want to go. You got to want to get there. There must be a deep desire to attain it. And then to the extent to which you believe in your ability to get there.

Now you may think, "Right now, I can't see any ability in me to get where I want to go. Do I deserve it? If it aligns with my values and my mission in my life, can I get it?"

No matter what has happened to you in your life or what bad decisions or poor choices you've made, the truth is that our past does not define us. It is a part of our history and a chapter in the storybook of our lives, but it is not what determines how we finish this life. It's imperative to be able to put your past in its proper perspective. As we have mentioned previously, you need to forgive others and yourself. Know that God fully forgives you as well, and move forward toward the new goals and dreams you have in your heart.

I have often said to my coaching clients, "You may think that God is through with you or that you have done something so bad you have lost God's favor, but that's just not true. God is a forgiving and loving God, and yes, you may have messed up Plan A, but He still has His ultimate purpose and plan for your life. It's just going to take Plan B or C or D now, and maybe a different path, but the game isn't over."

I like how the Apostle Paul put it. If anyone had a chance to blow it with bad choices and decisions (like killing Christians, arresting people, and torturing them for their faith!), it was Paul. But he knew that the Lord was not done with him and wanted to breathe that same truth into your life. This is what he said so beautifully in Philippians 3:13-14, "Brothers, I do not consider that I have made it my own. But one thing I do: forgetting what lies behind and straining forward to what lies ahead, I press on toward the goal for the prize of the upward call of God in Christ Jesus."

One of the most important aspects of goal setting and manifesting is that everything is created in the mind *first*. Initially, there is mental creation—you visualize it in your mind and see it as real. Then afterward comes the physical manifestation of your vision. If you see it in your mind first, then eventually, you can birth it into reality. See it in your mind so you can hold it in your hands.

People who get ahead in life, who thrive and not just survive and lead a life of achievement, do so because they have definite goals, and work hard every day to achieve them. They put all their energy, willpower, and effort into achieving the goal, whatever it is. They think about it every day of their lives. It gets them up in the morning, and it keeps them giving their best all day long. It's the last thing on their mind before they go to sleep at night. They know what they want, and they have a vision of what that looks like. By thinking about it morning, noon, and night, you will begin to move towards it and bringing it to fruition.

In his famous book, *Man's Search for Meaning*, Viktor Frankl, a psychologist who survived the Nazi concentration camps, shares a compelling and relevant message for us even today. He says, "when people have a purpose to their lives and goals to reach towards, it makes them accountable to life. You're not just here to soak up a few rays in the sun or to take up space on the planet here somewhere. That's not your purpose in life. When you have a purpose, when you understand what your purpose is, and then you have goals to reach towards, then you become now accountable for your life."

Your goals should be an extension of your purpose and mission statement. They reflect your deepest values, your unique talent, and your sense of mission. An effective goal will primarily focus on results and not so much on activity. A good goal will help you identify where you want to be and determine where you are. It will help you figure out how to get there, telling you when you have arrived.

Goal setting is the process of moving from where you are to where you want to be. You become the designer of your life when you write down your goals.

One thing your goals must do is fill you up with positive, intense, obsessive emotion. When you think about your goals, they must be something you want with all your heart. The more intensely you feel about a goal, the more assuredly it will be buried deep in your subconscious mind, which will then guide and direct you along the path to its fulfillment.

Earl Nightingale, radio personality, speaker, and author, said it best, "The more intensely we feel about an idea or a goal, the more assuredly the idea, buried deep in our subconscious, will direct us along the path to its fulfillment…whatever we plan in our subconscious mind and nourish with repetition and emotion will one day become reality…people with goals succeed because they know where they're going…success is the progressive realization of a worthy goal or idea."

Do you realize your thoughts are tangible things? Things that come to pass that you can see, touch, and experience? As you think, you create. The reality is that you become what you think about. Suppose you want to discover the infinite possibilities God gave you. In that case, you must find a goal big enough and exciting enough to challenge you to push beyond your limits, abilities, and talents to discover your true potential.

A great example of this is the story of one of my favorite golfers, Fred Couples. Fred is from the Redmond, WA area where I grew up, and his best friend, the CBS sports announcer, is Jim Nantz. Fred Couples and Jim Nantz were college roommates in the late 1970s at the University of Houston. Both of them grew up with a great love for golf.

Fred Couples had the dream from a young age of winning the Master's golf tournament. Jim Nantz had the dream of becoming a CBS sports announcer. They used to play-act together, that Fred won the Master's golf title and that Jim would interview Fred in the green room in Butler Cabin—where the winner receives the green jacket from the previous year's winner. A CBS sports announcer interviews them. They did this act frequently. They talked about it. They visualized it. They believed that event would happen to both of them one day.

Amazingly, fourteen years later, in 1992, the scene they had rehearsed over and over again in Taub Hall at the University of Houston played out in reality as the whole world was watching. Fred Couples won the Master's title. Tournament officials whisked him away to the famous Butler Cabin. There, CBS sports announcer, his dear and close friend, Jim Nantz, interviewed him. After the cameras stopped rolling, the two embraced one another with tears of joy in their eyes. They always knew it would be the Master's tournament that Fred Couples would win and that Jim Nantz would cover it for CBS.

Denny Hamlin knows the power of thought. Hamlin, a full-time NASCAR Cup Series driver for the Joe Gibbs Racing team, drives the No. 11 Toyota Camry and has won 44 NASCAR Cup Series races. When Denny Hamlin was in second grade, his goal for the future was to win the Daytona 500 with his friends from school on his pit crew. He wrote this down on paper at the age of seven in second grade just like this, "my work is to win the Daytona 500. My car would be red, white, and blue. If I do win the Daytona 500, I could win 1,000,000 dollars. The reason for this is because I love racing." Hamlin delivered on his goal in 2016 on his 11th attempt. He went on to win the Daytona 500 in 2019 and 2020 as well.

One of the most popular Hollywood actors during the late 1990s and 2000s was Jim Carrey. He so believed in goals and manifesting his dreams that he wrote himself a $10 million check in 1992 for "acting services rendered" and dated it three years in the future. He kept the check in his wallet. In November 1995, Carrey had the lead in the movie "Dumb and Dumber" for — you guessed it — $10 million.

I am a firm believer that God never gives you a dream that matches your budget, nor is He checking your bank account. He is most interested in your faith in Him. A really big goal is something bigger than you, something you know you cannot do on your own. It's when you pray for things that are impossible for you but more than possible for the Creator of the Universe. As it says in Luke 1:37, "For nothing will be impossible with God."

You will be at your best and happiest when you are pursuing, thinking, planning, working towards something you want to bring about that challenges you.

You may know the WHO, WHAT, WHERE, WHEN of your goal, but it's essential to realize that even if you have no idea of HOW you will achieve your goal, it's still necessary to create the goal. This knowledge motivates and energizes you to start moving in that direction. You have to trust God with the HOW.

He will provide your need and open up opportunities you cannot imagine.

1 Corinthians 9:24-25 says, "In a race everyone runs, but only one person gets first prize. So run your race to win. To win the contest you must deny yourselves many things that would keep you from doing your best. An athlete goes to all this trouble just to win a blue ribbon or a silver cup, but we do it for a heavenly reward that never disappears."

Your goals should revolve around each of these eight areas of your life:

- **Spiritual:** Relationship with God, morals, life purpose, stewardship, church

- **Family:** Parents, spouse, children, siblings, intimacy and sex, parents, relatives

- **Social:** Friends, community, environment, networking

- **Life Planning:** Finances, time, goals, life balance, life transitions, aging, mortality

- **Health:** Physical, nutrition, stress, lifestyle, emotional well-being, attitude

- **Personal Development:** Reading, learning, education, values, self-worth, beliefs

- **Fun/Recreation:** Vacation, hobbies, sports, travel, rest, fun, music, art, humor

- **Work:** Career, leadership, relations, skills, four quadrants, management, planning

I want you to write out **ONE THING** you want to do in each of those areas over the next 12 months.

Follow this guideline for each one of your goals. It will help you be very clear about what it is that you want to achieve.

- WHAT is the Goal:

- WHY is it important:
- What is your MOTIVE/INNER DRIVE:
- How will it be MEASURED:
- Date of completion:
- What will you GIVE/SACRIFICE in return:
- What might be your major challenges:
- Write on Paper a Plan of Action: Begin at the end, work your way backward
- Take Action NOW!

In the next chapter, we will discuss one of the most critical and challenging aspects of your life. You are either a slave or you are a driver of your destiny, but either way, mastering this part of your life will truly bring freedom to you.

Thinking About Setting Goals and Manifesting My Dreams

Every day look at these goals you've written down, visualize them and take time to think about them. I would recommend you take it a step further. Something that I do that has been very powerful is hanging a vision board. Put this in your house and place pictures of things that you want to accomplish on it. When you look at that every day, I'm telling you, it does powerful stuff for helping you to bring those things into reality every day.

Look at the goals you wrote down and the reason that you're committed to achieving them. You know the journey of a thousand miles begins with a single step. I want to encourage you with your goals, to take your dreams and make them become a reality.

Now I want you to think about your DREAMS. Write them down on a piece of paper like you did the goals. Take some time to do this. Let the creative process flow and write things that you've always wanted to do in your life. Because of limiting beliefs, you've always said to yourself, "*well, you know, I'll never be able to do that.*" Yeah, you're right. You never will. The more you say, "*I never will,*" or "*I can't*" or "*it won't happen,*" I guarantee you it won't. You're just talking yourself right out of seeing those things happen in your life. If you want something to happen, it's okay to dream big. I don't care how crazy a dream is, write it down and start thinking about how you're going to accomplish it.

16

Roadmap for Creating Financial Freedom in Your Life

"Financial freedom is a mental, emotional, and educational process."
Robert Kiyosaki, author, entrepreneur, inventor

"The real source of wealth and capital in this new era is not material things it is the human mind, the human spirit, the human imagination and our faith in the future. That's the magic of a free society everyone can move for- ward and prosper because wealth comes from within!"
Steve Forbes, Editor-in-Chief of Forbes Magazine

"Behold, what I have seen to be good and fitting is to eat and drink and find enjoyment in all the toil with which one toils under the sun the few days of his life that God has given him, for this is his lot. Everyone also to whom God

has given wealth and possessions and power to enjoy them, and to accept his lot and rejoice in his toil—this is the gift of God. For he will not much remember the days of his life because God keeps him occupied with joy in his heart."
Ecclesiastes 5:18-20 (ESV)

MONEY has a bad reputation with people who don't have it. It gets the blame for everything from wars to infidelity, from destroying friendships to wrecking families. In the minds of the masses, the more ways they can demonize money, the more validated they feel for not seeking their fortunes. Instead of seeing the positive ways that money can enhance the most important things in life like our health, family relationships, and friendships, most people would rather scorn money and tell you how it can destroy the things we hold closest to our hearts.

Don't listen to negative people who don't know any better. The truth is money is not the most important thing in life, but it will make the most important things in life so much better. It's true—money doesn't buy happiness. But it will make you more comfortable, open doors, create opportunities, and make the good things in your life even better. It may even save your life or the life of a loved one. Decide today to make money a bigger priority in your life. As the late Zig Ziglar said, "Money isn't everything ... but it ranks right up there with oxygen."

Even if you have a healthy view of money, did you know that money issues and debt can affect your health?

According to an Associated Press-AOL Health poll, people who say they suffer from high stress due to debt were much more likely to suffer from health problems than those who weren't dealing with money troubles. That study confirms what researchers have known for years: **Low incomes are linked to poor health, high levels of debt, and increased stress.**

About 27 percent of those in debt had ulcers or digestive tract problems, compared with 8 percent of those with low levels of debt stress, and 44 percent had migraines or other headaches, compared with 15 percent of people with low debt stress.

Research has shown that the less money people have, the more likely they are to suffer from certain diseases, including Type 2 diabetes and heart disease. In low-income households, the rates of obesity, hypertension, and high blood pressure are often higher than average. Many factors are to blame, but the fact remains: Money makes it easier to stay healthy.

My goal is to help you feel more comfortable about money, reverse the thinking that money is a harmful object, and help you envision how you can make more of it.

What is the Definition of Wealth?

True wealth is a person's tangible and intangible assets: money, material possessions, and resources, as well as love, time, relationships, purpose-filled life, and health.

Financial wealth is a person's ability to survive "x" number of days forward. If you stopped working today, how long could you survive?

Wealth measures how much money your money is making. Wealth is a measure of cash flow from your asset column compared with the expense column. How much income do your assets produce?

Examples of liabilities, otherwise known as debt, include mortgages, credit card balances, student loans, and car loans. An individual's assets, meanwhile, include checking and savings account balances, the value of securities such as stocks or bonds, real property value, the market value of an automobile, cash value of permanent insurance, etc. After selling all assets and paying off personal debt is the net worth.

Question: Can you have a net worth in the millions of dollars and still be broke?

Yes, you can be holding significant investments in real property, stock, bonds, ETF (Stock Exchange-Traded Fund), mutual funds, coins, gold, and silver. However, until you sell these investments and have cash in hand, then you are still broke. That is why we call them paper assets. Suppose something happens to the housing or stock market, or an event that causes an economic turndown or crash. In that case, your paper assets may be gone. If you didn't have anything in cash, you might die poor even though your net worth was millions of dollars. Net worth is the value of the assets a person owns, minus the liabilities they owe.

Real wealth is when your cash flow exceeds your expenses. Visualize this scenario for a moment: You wake up at 5 am, make the bed, brush your teeth, spend some time reading, personal development, exercise at the gym, have a nice breakfast, and at 8 am you do not have to go anywhere or do anything because your assets are generating a net cash flow for you that exceeds your monthly expenses. That, my friends, is what real wealth is— assets producing cash flow greater than your expenses.

The issue with money in the Bible isn't really about being rich and prosperous financially. The Bible says that it can be one of God's great blessings upon us. The real issue is about **ownership, attitude,** and the **motives of your heart** with the money you have.

Let's review some of the scripture around this issue. Deuteronomy 8:18 says, "You shall remember the Lord your God, for it is He who gives you power to get wealth, that He may confirm His covenant that He swore to your fathers, as it is this day." And in Proverbs 3:9-10, we read, "Honor the Lord with your wealth and with the first-fruits of all your produce; then your barns will be filled with plenty, and your vats will be bursting with wine."

And Psalm 112:1-3 reads, "Blessed is the man who fears the Lord, who finds great delight in His commands. Wealth and riches are in his house, and his righteousness endures forever."

One thing is for sure, a lack of money is not the problem; it is merely a symptom of what's going on inside you. Financial success starts in your mind. You have to do the following:

* Know what you want

* Why does it matter to you?

* Believe it's possible for you

* Who must you become to attain it

* Believe you deserve it

* Focus on it by thinking and visualizing it

* Be willing to pay the price to get it

There are outer laws of money, and there are inner laws of money. The outer laws include things like business knowledge, money management, and investment strategies. And while these are important for sure, the inner game is more important. Your income can grow only to the same level at which you grow personally.

You see, the issue of money boils down to this: it's our understanding of, our education in, and our associations with money that will determine if it is our friend or foe in this life. In my experience, having success with money and building financial freedom takes focus, courage, knowledge, expertise, 100 percent of your effort, a never-give-up attitude, and, of course, a healthy money mindset.

Modern Day Myths About Money

Myth 1—Money will make you happy...Money doesn't equal happiness. Money is neutral; it's a tool to use to get what you want out of life. Ask the thousands of people who have won a lottery how happy they are. If your mindset is not correct, no amount of money is ever going to fix that.

Myth 2—Money will change you...Money is a great revealer of who you are. If you are greedy, more money will just make you greedier. If you have a scarcity mentality, you become even a more self-centered, self-important person. You won't share or bless others with your prosperity. If you have an abundance mentality, then your view will be to make it grow, bless and help others, and maximize the benefits of your prosperity. Again, if your mindset is not right about money, no amount of money is ever going to fix that.

Myth 3—Wealth makes people bad and selfish...Money is a very neutral thing. It's a tool to use in exchange for value for something else. It's neither good nor bad; it's neither positive nor negative. Money in and of itself doesn't make people bad or selfish. How you handle money has a lot to do with how your parents raised you and their example.

KEY POINT OF DISCUSSION: We tend to be identical to one or a combination of our parents in the area of money, finances, and mindsets.

Read the words and phrases below. Did you hear your family say any of these about money?

- *Money is the root of all evil*
- *Money doesn't grow on trees*
- *You can't be spiritual and rich*
- *The rich get richer and the poor get poorer*
- *Money isn't for people like us*
- *We can't afford it*
- *Do I look like I am made of money?*
- *They were born with a silver spoon in their mouth*
- *Haven't got a penny to my name*
- *Money makes the world go round*
- *Penny pincher*
- *Living on a shoestring budget*

- *Time is money*

- *Go after it before someone takes it from you*

Another aspect affecting your money mindset is your parents' example; how they relate to money and how that was communicated to you. Did they manage or mismanage it? Were they spenders or savers? Did they invest or not? Were they risk-takers, or did they play it safe with money? Did the money come easy, or was it a struggle? Was there joy or arguing over money in your home growing up?

Finally, the personal experiences you have determines a lot of how you view money itself, people who have it or don't, and what people spend their money on in your sphere of influence. Perhaps you knew or worked for people with money—they either gave you a positive or negative perspective about money subconsciously. Maybe you have worked with poor or homeless people, and that too may have subconsciously given you a positive or negative outlook. What personal experiences have you had that shaped your perspective on finances and money?

I want to encourage you to get your hands on one of the best sources of understanding money, mindset, and the impacts your life experience has had on how you relate to money today. Author T. Harv Eker's book *Secrets of the Millionaire Mind* will help you drill down deep within yourself of **WHY** you have the beliefs about money and prosperity that you do. Now, back to our myths…

Myth 4—It is better to give than to receive… The more you receive, the more you have to share. The best way to always help the poor and needy is not to end up where they are. The Bible promotes giving and receiving. Answer this question for yourself, 'Which comes first, the giving or receiving?'

Myth 5—Getting out of debt is the path to financial freedom… This myth is a serious area of confusion for many people today. You'll see many different takes on this. Dave Ramsey (and his hundreds of coaches) and Chris Hogan believe in paying everything off, including your mortgage. On the other hand, Grant Cardone, Robert Kiyosaki, and many other business-minded people believe debt is acceptable as long as it develops cash flow for you. Using other people's money—like banks and lenders to acquire assets—just makes more sense than using your own money.

To me, there is a middle ground between the two schools of thought. Of course, having a credit card or revolving debt with high-interest rates makes no sense and will keep you poor forever. There should be a balance between paying off debts and investing in cash flow-producing assets. The challenge comes from being out of debt, but you still have to pay income tax, property taxes, adjust for inflation, and somehow, make your money grow in a tax-favored manner. You can be debt-free and be broke if you earn and burn your money and not produce and protect by focusing on keeping what you make.

There are so many things a person can do to better themselves financially. Some of those include creating corporations, hiring a great tax strategy accountant to help from overpaying on taxes, investing in yourself as your greatest asset, improving your skillsets, increasing your networks, and investing in your business.

Myth 6—I can save money to create wealth...Let's be honest here, very few people can save themselves into wealth, and usually, savers end up the losers. Today's average American believes they will get wealthy by saving money through instruments such as mutual funds, 401(k) plans, retirement plans, stocks, bonds, etc. Over the last 20 years, the average return on the S&P 500 is between 5-7%. Financial professionals tell us to figure out what your number is to live comfortably for x number of years. Usually, the figure is in the millions of dollars for most people. The challenge with this mindset and this line of thinking is that people don't figure in the **top three wealth destroyers:**

Management fees take about 4-5% of your total savings. **Taxes** which include income, state, and local take a huge chunk as well.

Inflation over time, everything cost more in the future.

Your nest egg becomes dramatically smaller after these three get added to the equation.

We will get into this more when you attend the *Power to Thrive* workshops and coaching program, but please understand **Wall Street has four basic rules** when it comes to your money:

1. They want your money very badly!

2. They want your money systematically

3. They want to hold onto your money for as long as they possibly can

4. They will give your money back to you very slowly and as little as possible

Over 20 years from December 31, 1993, through December 31, 2013, the S&P 500 returned an average annual return of 9.28%. But the average mutual fund investor made just over 2.54%, according to Dalbar, one of the leading industry research firms. That's an 80% difference!

Think about it, Wall Street takes no risk, they invest none of their capital on their part, and they get to enjoy a gain of 85% or better at your expense! Numbers don't lie, and math is the path to real financial freedom. Those who do the math and focus on cash flow are usually the big winners in creating wealth for themselves.

In the parable of the talents in Matthew 25:14-30, even the Lord Jesus Christ Himself makes this point very clear. The man who tried to save his money, bury it and preserve it was the one Jesus condemned. The other two people, who took the money and multiplied it, were given more and commended for their actions.

Another book I highly recommend you purchase is *MONEY Master the Game: 7 Simple Steps to Financial Freedom* by Tony Robbins. This book has a gold mine of moneymaking information. It lays out secrets from the world's greatest financial minds. It's like a *Think and Grow Rich* book but for money and investing. It includes interviews with 50 of the most legendary financial experts in the world.

Myth 7—Investing is too complicated; I need advisors to help me... This myth is what Wall Street and the big investment companies want you to believe. They convince people that the only way to higher returns and income growth is to increase risk, give up control, and defer taxes way down the road. They want you to believe that you are too dumb to manage your finances and that you need to leave it with someone with a fancy title or specialized education who can do better with your money than you can. They tell you to play the long game, which enriches them and allows them to use your money for their gains. But I believe in 'Occam's razor,' which says "entities should not be multiplied without necessity," or more simply, the simplest explanation is usually the right one. I have learned from personal experience that the easier the explanation, the simpler you can make something, the better it is for everyone, especially when it comes to money, investing, and growing cash-flowing assets. The road to financial freedom is not complicated; you just need to educate yourself and build up your skillsets to make it happen.

Myth 8—There is a shortage of money... The truth is if you do not develop the proper skills and financial education, money will not do you much good at all. It will come into your hands and leave just as fast. When you commit your life to education, knowledge, learning from those who are where you want to be and seeing money for what it truly is, you can multiply and increase it when you have it. Remember, it's about the exchange of value; just ask those who have harnessed that principle like those in the billionaire bracket. The more value your business or service provides, the more money multiplies. A scarcity mental-ity embraces this myth which promotes greed, hoarding, and a non-giving mindset.

Proverbs 3:3-16: "Blessed is the man who finds wisdom, the man who gains understanding, for wisdom is more profitable than silver and yields better returns than gold...Long life is in her right hand; in her left hand are riches and honor."

Since we have covered the myths surrounding money, now is an excellent time to explain the difference between *investing* and *speculation.* By definition, investing is when you part with capital in the expectation of safety of principal and an adequate return in the form of a dividend, interest, rent, or cash flow. Investing allows more control, lower risk, multiple ways to make money, and accountability and results. Things like rental properties, buy-ing an established and profitable business, and cash value life insurance are investments.

Speculation, on the other hand, is very much like gambling. It's the purchase of an asset, hoping that it will become more valuable in a short period of time. It's the assumption of unusual business risk in hopes of obtaining commensurate gain. A speculative investor is less concerned about the value of security because their focus is on price movements. Annual income the asset might bring in (such as dividends, interest, or cash flow) is not a priority at all. What interests this kind of investor is the price for which they can sell the given financial instrument on a future date. Things like stocks, 401(k), hedge funds, IPOs (Initial Public Offering), and venture capital are speculation and are much like playing the roulette wheel in Las Vegas.

An *investment* is an asset or item acquired to generate income or appreciation in the future. *Speculation* is a financial transaction with a substantial risk of losing all value but expecting a sig-nificant gain. This may surprise you, but many people, maybe even you, are speculating about your financial future rather than investing. That's why the lies of "trading time for money," "retire-ment is a 40+ year plan," and "there are so many ups and downs in the market" are dangerous—you can reach retirement age and not have the funds you envisioned.

There are **four key factors** to making money investing. If you want to be financially free, then all your investments must have these four:

Appreciation-Growth. Is there growth over time, will the asset increase in value? Will the assets produce income without diminishing their value?

Cash Flow; is most important. Passive income independent of the market's ups and downs and does not require 100% of your effort. It makes you money no matter what.

Tax Benefits. There is a big difference between eliminating tax and deferring tax. When you defer tax, all you're doing is just kicking the can down the road for a future time. And if you think about it, why would you want to do that when there's too much unpredictability? Nobody knows what the tax laws or rates will be in the future. When you withdraw money from tax-deferred accounts, it is taxed as ordinary income in the calendar year in which you make the withdrawal. Suppose you need extra funds for a vacation, purchasing a new car, or helping a family member. In that case, the excess funds withdrawn might bump you into a higher tax bracket. You could find yourself paying 25 cents in taxes or more on each dollar you withdraw.

Withdrawals affect Social Security taxation as well. In addition to withdrawals from tax-deferred accounts taxed as ordinary income, they can also affect how much of your Social Security income is taxed. Each withdrawal may make more of your Social Security income subject to taxation. There is a formula that determines how much of your Social Security is taxed. One of the components of this formula is the amount of "other income" you have. Additional IRA (Individual Retirement Account) withdrawals increase other income and may cause more of your Social Security income to be taxed. A few retirees find they pay over 40 cents in taxes per dollar of IRA withdrawals because their IRA withdrawals cause more of their Social Security to be taxed.

I am a big proponent of hiring a good tax strategist who can give you strategy and understands tax codes and laws so that you can minimize tax as much as legally and ethically possible. Like the mechanics used to say on the old FRAM oil filter commercial, "You can pay me NOW, or you can pay me LATER." Deferring income to me sounds more like speculating and gambling than actual investing and tax strategy.

Leverage. Using other people's money to purchase income-producing assets and collapse time. You also leverage yourself by hiring coaches to help you grow, adding employees and staff, and technology to help you be more efficient and system-oriented.

Believe it or not, there are only three primary investments in the world today that have all four of these pillars, and it's not the stock market, mutual funds, 401(k) plans, bonds. The only three that have all four of these pillars are owning a business, real estate, and cash value life insurance.

To learn more about this, please go to www.Cashflowtactics. com. If you want basic financial education that makes sense and help putting together a game plan to be financially free in 10 years or less, please check them out.

16 Principles for Creating Financial Freedom

Wealth Begins with Desire: If you don't want it bad enough, it does not come to you. You will need to desire wealth with all your being. What we focus on expands.

Develop a Cash Flow Mindset vs. Net Worth Mindset: Net worth is important as a scorecard. But whether you're an individual or a business, cash flow is more vital. If you're worth millions, but you're bleeding out cash, it's only a matter of time before you hit financial ruin. Likewise, if your net worth is low, but your net cash flow is high, you have plenty to keep you afloat each month, and you can build net worth.

Know the difference between an asset and a liability: Assets put money in your pocket, and liabilities take money out! The big mistake many people make today is spending their lives buying liabilities instead of assets. Common liabilities include cars, vacations, clothes, eating out, unused subscriptions, etc. If you haven't read the book *Rich Dad, Poor Dad* by Robert Kiyosaki yet, do. It will give you a fresh and different perspective on money matters and the basics of wealth accumulation.

Control Spending with a Budget: Know your numbers and live within your means. A budget is a cash flow manager for you. It helps you stay in control of your money and how it comes in and how it goes out. The real benefit is that it can help you save money instead of overspending and enables you to make the most of every dollar you earn or bring in. It is a tool to help you better control and manage what you have coming in month-to-month.

Think in terms of investing and not in terms of lifestyle or material things: You are either a producer or a consumer. Plain and straightforward, producers invest, and consumers spend.

Develop an emergency account with $5k - 10k in it: This is a great way to develop peace of mind and give yourself a lot of control. Emergency funds create a financial buffer that can keep you afloat in a time of need without having to rely on credit cards or high-interest loans. It's essential to have an emergency fund if you have debt because it can help you avoid borrowing more. It comes in handy for things like medical issues, car fixes, unforeseen home repairs, losing a job, etc.

Gain Control of the Mother of All Debt, High-interest Credit: Credit cards with balances and high-interest rates can zap a person's ability to grow cash flow. Interest rates on credit cards can be high. Every single loan, whether installment like auto and mortgages or student loans, all have interest tied to them. The national average annual percentage rate (APR) is currently over 16% on credit cards and 8% on student loans. The danger on credit cards is that the interest on them compounds, so the longer you wait to pay off the balance, the more you'll owe in interest. Best practices on higher interest, pay off the balance each month to avoid paying the high interest.

Remember Proverbs 22:7, "The rich rules over the poor, and the borrower is the slave of the lender."

Implement the 10-20-70 Principle: 10% to charity or tithe, 20% to investment fund so you can purchase cash flowing opportunities, and live on the remaining 70%. The key here is to give first, help yourself second, pay everyone and everything else after that.

Reference Luke 6:38, "Give, and it will be given to you. Good measure, pressed down, shaken together, running over, will be put into your lap. For with the same measure that you use, it will be measured back to you."

Understand the Power of Compound Interest: Compound interest means that you begin to earn interest on the interest you receive, which multiplies your money at an accelerating rate. In other words, if you have $500 and earn 10% in interest, you have $550. Then, if you earn 10% of interest on that, you end up with $605. And so on, until eventually, your original $500 will eclipse the amount of interest you have gained.

Three main factors influence the rate at which your money compounds:

The interest rate you earn on your investment or the profit you make.

Time left to grow. The more time you give your money to build upon itself, the more it compounds.

The tax rate and the date you have to pay taxes on your interest. You will end up with far more money if you don't have to pay taxes at all or until the end of the compounding period rather than at the end of each year.

Buy insurance to protect your assets: Protection can be in the form of Life insurance, Disability Income, Health, Auto & Home, Umbrella, Commercial, Long Term Care, and more. Insurance is the wall built around you and your earning potential, your businesses, your material assets and possessions, and to protect yourself against losing everything for which you have worked. It just makes sense, pennies on the dollar out of your pocket vs. having insurance pay for the loss. Smart people carry lots of insurance. To make sure you are not overpaying for coverage and still very much protected, I recommend you visit me at *www.CavanessInsuranceAgency.com*

Develop Numerous Streams of Income: The obvious ones are real estate and business acquisitions. Both take training and developing skill sets to master. But the new term these days is "side hustle" income—making money outside of your normal job or career. Side hustles include writing, virtual assistant, videography, Uber, coaching, Fiverr, blogging, podcasting, YouTube, speaking, Airbnb, affiliate marketing, tutoring, network marketing, or a social media influencer who creates online information about products.

I highly recommend you read the book *The Side Hustle Bible* by Jacob Wallace. He has over 150 ideas on making a few hundred to thousands of dollars a month doing something outside of your regular employment.

Don't let your emotions get the best of you, and make financial decisions wisely: Math is the path, and numbers don't lie. With any investment, take the emotion out of the equation and let the numbers speak the story. It either makes sense, or it doesn't. Frequently, fear, guilt, insecurity, anxiety, jealousy, regret, sadness, and over-confidence are as much as 2x more powerful than positive emotions when making money decisions.

Write out financial goals and create a plan of action: Hopefully, you have been doing this from the chapter on goal setting and manifesting. You have to see it in your mind first before you hold it in your hand. The key is implementing a game plan, based on 90-day periods of time. Think about it, you can be financially free in ten years or less, but it takes a goal, a big WHY on your part, and a step-by-step plan of action to set everything in motion.

Use the tax codes to reduce and limit taxes legally and ethically: Please know this, the tax code was not written for employees or even, in most cases, self-employed people; it is for business owners. Having a great accountant who knows more than just filing tax returns can be worth tens of thousands of dollars in savings to you. Having a quarterly tax strategy (or at least every six months) will help you plan instead of being caught off guard and surprised at the end of the year. This way, more money is staying in your pocket and not going to the government.

Under pay for investments and overpay for developing good team members: Your best investment will be in people—building a team, having others beside you to go along for the ride. Hire slow, fire fast, pay your people well, and treat them with respect. Empower them with being a vital part of the team; they are an invaluable asset to you. Nobody has ever built anything of significance without the help of others. Teamwork is the lynchpin to creating financial freedom.

Find a Personal Coach or Role Model: All truly successful people hire a coach in the area they want to build or develop skills. Coaches are one of the best investments you will ever make, one of the best ROI decisions you will ever make. They help you get to where you want to go faster, better and help prevent costly mistakes and lose money. With my background and expertise in coaching, pastoring, business ownership, and training, I can help you get where you want to go with your life. Visit **RichCavaness. com** to get started, and order my book, *Next Level Living: Every Christian Needs a Coach in Life*

Lastly, before we wrap up this chapter, let me encourage you to come up with your number for financial freedom. You should clearly understand the 'gap' between where you are today and where you want to be in ten years or less. This number is unique to you and should take care of your monthly savings, basic needs, and lifestyle.

Use the following as a template, and I will give an example beside each entry to demonstrate. Where you see dollar amounts in this example, you will need to replace them with the numbers specific to your situation.

Income you want to make to provide your Lifestyle = $100,000

Minus (8%) Employment Taxes = $8,000

Minus (30%) Federal Income Taxes = $30,000

Minus (5%) State Income Taxes = $5,000

After-Tax Income = $57,000

Minus Annual Savings = $3,000

Minus Employment Expenses (car, clothes, tools, etc.) = $6,000

Your number to reach financial freedom = $48,000

Take that number and divide it by 12. This is how much you need to create in monthly cash flow to become financially free = **$4,000 per month**

If you are like me, this number is much smaller than you initially thought, and it seems much more attainable and doable. I hope this inspires you to aspire to rise above your circumstances, believe you can do this, and live a life of financial freedom in ten years or less.

Congratulations on making it this far through the *Power to Thrive* journey! The last chapter is the absolute key to everything in the *Power to Thrive* coaching system, where the power in your life ultimately comes. I will teach you how to ignite it fully so you can live, breathe, and prosper in every area of your life according to God's purpose and plan for you.

Thinking About My Money Mindset and Financial Freedom

What did you experience when you were young with money, wealth, poverty, and finances?

What beliefs and habits did each of your parents display regarding money and finances?

How has this modeling affected your financial life and your marriage today and in the past?

Which of the 16 Principles for Creating Financial Freedom can you implement immediately and make the most significant difference in your life today?

What do you want today in your life in the area of money? Write down some general goals, and some attitude changes you can make, and some of the beliefs you know to be true where finances are concerned.

17

Six Actions to Ignite God's Power in Your Life

"There is more power in one word from God
than all the power of the enemy."
Sid Roth, evangelist, TV host, Jewish crusader

"For God has not given us a spirit of fear, but of
power and of love and of a sound mind."
2 Timothy 1:7 (NKJV)

Swedish inventor Alfred Nobel established the Nobel prizes. Besides being the namesake behind one of the most prestigious awards for academic, cultural, and scientific achievements, Nobel is also well-known for making it possible for people to blow things up.

Alfred Nobel was an engineer and inventor who constructed bridges and buildings in his nation's capital of Stockholm. It was his construction work that inspired Nobel to research new methods of blasting rock. Nobel started experimenting with an explosive chemical substance called nitroglycerin which led to the invention of dynamite.

Italian chemist Ascanio Sobrero first invented nitroglycerin in 1846. In its natural liquid state, nitroglycerin is very volatile. Nobel understood this, and in 1866, he discovered that mixing nitroglycerin with silica would turn the liquid into a malleable paste called dynamite. One advantage that dynamite had over nitroglycerin was that it could be cylinder-shaped for insertion into the drilling holes used for mining.

In 1863, Nobel invented the detonator, or blasting cap, for detonating nitroglycerin. The detonator used a strong shock rather than heat combustion to ignite the explosives. The Nobel Company built the first factory to manufacture nitroglycerin and dynamite.

In 1867, Nobel received the US patent number 78,317 for his invention of dynamite. To detonate the dynamite rods, Nobel also improved his detonator or blasting cap so that it ignited by lighting a fuse. In 1875, Nobel invented blasting gelatin, which was more stable and robust than dynamite and patented it in 1876. In 1887, the French granted him a patent for *"ballistite,"* a smokeless blasting powder made from nitrocellulose and nitro-glycerin. Even though Nobel created ballistite as a substitute for black gunpowder, a variation is still used today as a solid fuel rocket propellant.

One thing that greatly disturbed Alfred Nobel was his dyna-mite invention's adverse effects on humanity and the world. He feared his legacy would be the inventor of dynamite—a substance known for being destructive and hurting and killing people. So just one year before he died in 1896, Nobel stipulated in his last will and testament that 94% of his total assets go toward the cre-ation of an endowment fund to honor achievements in physical science, chemistry, medical science or physiology, literary work and service toward peace. Hence, the Nobel prize is awarded yearly to people whose work helps humanity.

One of the most encouraging aspects of God's love for you is that He gives you supernatural power to live for Him. It's not your power or your strength; it's His power and strength working through us and in us.

As mentioned previously in Chapter 7, The word Power used in the New Testament is *"dunamis,"* from which we derive the word dynamite. The Greek meaning for power is might, full of strength, abundance, miraculous power. This is precisely what God wants to give us if we will only let him. Notice how the following Bible verses tell you where the power comes from:

Micah 3:8, "But truly I am full of Power by the Spirit of the Lord, and of justice and might."

Hebrews 4:12, "For the word of God is living and powerful, and sharper than any two-edged sword, piercing even to the division of soul and spirit, and of joints and marrow, and is a discerner of the thoughts and intents of the heart."

Ephesians 3:20, "Now to Him who is able to do exceedingly abundantly above all that we ask or think, according to the power that works in us."

Acts 4:33, "And with great power the apostles gave witness to the resurrection of the Lord Jesus. And great grace fell upon them all."

Acts 6:8, "And Stephen, full of faith and power, did great wonders and signs among the people."

Luke 9:1, "Then He called His twelve disciples together and gave them power and authority over all demons, and to cure diseases. He sent them to preach the kingdom of God and to heal the sick."

Luke 10:19, "Behold, I give you authority to trample on serpents and scorpions, and over all the power of the enemy, and nothing shall by any means hurt you."

Luke 24:49, "Behold, I send the Promise of My Father upon you; but tarry in the city of Jerusalem until you are endued with power from on high."

So if you want *true* power and the energy, explosiveness, and magnitude of dynamite, then you need to tap into God's power for your life.

Six actions to igniting God's power in your life

1. *You will need to know who God is to you.* He is for you, with you, and always desires the best for you. He designed you for a unique and special purpose. How you understand and experience the God of all creation will massively determine whether you experience the fullness of God's power in your life. That's why the first three chapters in *Power to Thrive* are critical for you in your relationship with the Lord.

2. *Surrender to His power and let God work through you.* Most people naturally tend to think that power comes from force or manipulation. But in God's realm, power comes through surrender, exercising humility, and letting God lead and direct your life. It's about getting out of your own way and letting God guide your steps.

3. *Walk in God's ways and following His Word.* It's very unpopular today to follow the wisdom, history, and guidance of a book written thousands of years ago. To many, the Bible is an outdated, unreliable, division-causing manuscript. As a follower of God, you have some choices to make regarding the Bible. I allude to this later when we talk about the three types of people alive today, still, the Bible is either the words of God Himself directed by the Holy Spirit, or it's just historical fiction. If indeed it's God's spoken word to every single person in the world, then carefully consider what is inside the Bible and how it applies to your life and relationship with God.

4. *Learn from others by reading, listening, watching those who have gone before you.* One of the great principles of life is to learn from the mistakes and successes, valleys and peaks of others who have gone before us. Other people's mentorship, counsel, and coaching can have a profound impact on your life. I love to read books and articles from other Christian leaders and followers. Having Christian role models in your life—people who live a godly example in this world today—can have a profound and powerful influence on your life.

5. *Walk in faith and courage; expect miracles and big things to happen.* You must not discount God's ability to accomplish the impossible. Two of the greatest principles you read throughout the entirety of the Bible, from Genesis to Revelation, are summed up like this: **"Do not be afraid and trust in the Lord with all your heart."** The enemy of God is responsible for fear and doubt. That's why reading the Bible is so important. It allows you to read the stories, see the history, and see how God has led His people through thousands of years. It builds up your faith and trust in the God of all the universe.

6. *Be in a state and season of prayer always, seeking His guidance and wisdom.* So much has been made to complicate prayer with mechanical aspects that many people have turned away from it. But if you know who God is to you, if you have chosen to let God lead you and trust in His ways, then why not talk, think, and ponder His goodness all the time? God wants to reveal Himself to you, and He listens and directs you because of His great love for you.

Mark 11:34 says, "Therefore I say to you, whatever things you ask when you pray, believe that you receive them, and you will have them."

You may have heard it said, "knowledge is power." If you incorporate these six steps, you will be well on your way to gaining power. Knowledge may be acquired from any of these steps and then converted into power by organizing them into definite plans and then by taking action on those plans. The power in knowledge only comes when you develop a plan of action to implement what you have learned. In James 1:22, the Bible says, "But be **DOERS** of the word, and not hearers only, deceiving yourselves." Action is a key element in igniting God's power in your life.

Ultimately, to experience God's power, the Holy Spirit of God must continually fill you. The Holy Spirit enables us to live the Christian life as God intends and gives us the power to do what we can't on our own and to live out our God's intended purpose and plan. To understand the who, what, where, when, why, and how of the Holy Spirit of God, read the book of John, chapters 14, 15, and 16. In those chapters, John answers these questions along with others you may have. Below you will find the specific functions and description of the purpose of the Holy Spirit:

The Holy Spirit is to be with us and by our side and help us.

The Holy Spirit is the truth that comes from God and will lead us into that truth.

The Holy Spirit came to dwell in us and testify of Jesus Christ.

The Holy Spirit will teach us and bring things to our remembrance about God.

The Holy Spirit came to convict the world of sin, righteousness, and justice.

The Holy Spirit came to glorify Jesus Christ.

The Holy Spirit confirms our relationship with God.

Although the Holy Spirit lives within all Christians, not all Christians are directed and empowered by the Holy Spirit. Not all Christians experience the Holy Spirit's power. The Bible says that there are three kinds of people in the world — the natural person, the spiritual person, and the worldly Christian.

The natural person—These persons have not yet trusted Christ's death to pay for their sins. Therefore, Christ does not yet live in them, and the Bible is just an old, outdated, unreliable, flawed manuscript in their thinking. Natural persons direct their own life since they have not yet recognized Jesus as Lord nor the Bible as their handbook for life.

The spiritual person—These persons have trusted Christ as their Savior and Lord and are trusting the Holy Spirit to direct and empower them moment by moment. These persons, therefore, yield fully to Holy Spirit's direction, knowing their life now belongs to Jesus Christ. They trust Him fully; they think and feel like Him. Their priorities are His as well. They live in obedience to God's ways and not those of the world. The Bible is their constitution for living; it's their handbook for life.

The worldly Christian—this is the most dangerous person of the three, believe it or not. These persons have trusted Christ to pay for their sins but still seek to live the Christian life in their strength rather than God's. They live in their human strength instead of having the Spirit of God empowering or directing them. They see the Bible as optional and not overly important, only referenced when they need it to prove a belief or to make a point to someone else. It's more of a trophy piece that sits on the table or on a shelf that collects dust and is more of a monument than the living, breathing words of the Creator of the Universe.

A worldly Christian person does not trust God enough to let the Holy Spirit direct every aspect of their life. Instead, they seek to remain in charge of deciding the what, where, when, and how of their life journey. There tends to be strife, envy, and division among them and their brothers and sisters in Jesus Christ. Worldly powers of media, sports, Hollywood, financial systems and institutions, fashion, universities, and educational systems influence them more than the Holy Spirit of God.

Jesus Christ himself specifically addressed this group of worldly Christians in his address to the seven churches in the book of Revelation. He refers to worldly Christians as "luke-warm" and having a perceived need of nothing today because they have their basic needs taken care of:

> "I know your works, that you are neither cold nor hot. I could wish you were cold or hot. So then, because you are lukewarm, and neither cold nor hot, I will vomit you out of My mouth. Because you say, 'I am rich, have become wealthy, and have need of nothing'—and do not know that you are wretched, miserable, poor, blind, and naked— I counsel you to buy from Me gold refined in the fire, that you may be rich; and white garments, that you may be clothed, that the shame of your nakedness may not be revealed; and anoint your eyes with eye salve, that you may see. As many as I love, I rebuke and chasten. Therefore be zealous and repent. Behold, I stand at the door and knock. If anyone hears My voice and opens the door, I will come in to him and dine with him, and he with Me. To him who overcomes I will grant to sit with Me on My throne, as I also overcame and sat down with My Father on His throne. He who has an ear, let him hear what the Holy Spirit says to the churches." Revelation 3:15-22

The abundant Christian life is the Christ-directed life by which Christ lives His life in and through us in the power of the Holy Spirit. We can be filled with the Holy Spirit by trusting God to produce in us the fruitful life he has promised as we live for Him.

In October 2005, Carrie Underwood released her huge cross-over hit, "Jesus Take the Wheel." It's a great metaphor that helps us understand what it means to be empowered by our Helper, the Holy Spirit. We can picture our life as being a car; when we invite Jesus Christ into our life, He comes in and sits in the driver's seat, and the Holy Spirit takes the wheel. He is the best driver, and He knows the way we should follow. But time and time again, we think we know better, so we take back the wheel. When we realize that we have done so, we need to move over and let Him take it back. When the Holy Spirit of God empowers us, He is the driver of our life, and we are His passengers in the car of life, and God is leading our way.

Just as Alfred Nobel created dynamite, a history-changing explosive element, you, too, have a power greater than dynamite living inside of you through the power of the Holy Spirit. God's desire for you is to have that Power. He desires for you to be full of strength, abundance, and miraculous power. God wants to share all this power with you if you will only let Him. Follow the six actions outlined in this chapter and ask for the gift of the Holy Spirit to be living inside of you so you can have the *Power to Thrive*, escape mediocrity, and elevate your everyday living.

Thinking About How to Release God's Power in Your Life

Which of the six action steps is the biggest challenge for you and why?

Which of the three persons described in this chapter do you relate to today?

What are some action steps you can take today to become a more spiritual person?

How would your life look different if you allowed God's power through the Holy Spirit to direct and guide your life?

Bringing Everything Full Circle

3 Simple Steps: Your Power to Thrive Checklist for Success

Here's a quick checklist to use anytime you want to see where you are and what still needs tweaking. This list helps you move towards freedom from mediocrity, unleashing God's power in your life, and living every day the best that you can. Take a look at the three simple steps and make sure that you not only understand them but that you have put a plan together and put forth action to make them happen in your life.

Step 1: Knowing your identity is the key to thriving in life.

1. Re-read the Thriver's Manifesto and print it out or take a picture so you can look at it every day.

2. Are you able with confidence to answer the four great questions of life?

3. Which identity is guiding your life today: personal, family, social, or God?

4. Did you list your top 10 values?

5. Has your WHY for your life become more apparent in your mind?

6. How many years of life do you have left, and what will you do to leave a legacy?

7. What have you identified as your primary spiritual gift? How will you use it?

8. What has changed about your view of God?

Step 2: Your outer world is a direct reflection of your inner world

1. Make a decision today to accept responsibility for your life and acknowledge that you have possession of the greatest gift in the universe: the power to choose.

2. How will having a growth mindset change the course of your life?

3. What fear is holding you back and why? What steps do you need to take to break out of your comfort zone?

4. Have you addressed your top three limiting beliefs and replaced them with empowering beliefs?

5. Have you acknowledged your need for forgiveness with God and asked Him to save your life?

Step 3: Physical and mental health will lead to emotional well-being

1. Have you walked yourself through the nine steps to forgiveness?

2. How will operating within your circle of control help lower stress in your life?

3. What steps have you taken to implement time chunking into your life?

4. Have you written down your goals and put a plan of action together to accomplish them?

5. Which myth about money has dominated your life? What has been its impact?

6. Which of the 16 principles of financial freedom will be a game-changer for you?

7. Have you identified what is holding you back from receiving the Holy Spirit's power in its fullness?

This list- is a quick overview for maximizing the pages you have just read. If there is anything you've missed, give yourself the gift of going back and reabsorbing it. Remember, repetition is the mother of skill development. Action is where all your power lives. This list is not everything you need, but it's a great checklist to trigger you to keep growing and implementing the lessons. Take the knowledge you learned and execute. Just make a little progress each day of the week, and before you know it, your path to thriving in life and escaping the prison of mediocrity will be reality.

I look forward to meeting you in person or virtually some-day soon. I hope you will take advantage of the Power to Thrive coaching system to partner in helping you live the life of your dreams. Until then, rise up, keep moving forward, employ the power of God, and live life with the enthusiasm it deserves.

If this book has been a blessing to you, help me get this mes-sage and content out to the world **posting a review on Amazon for me.** Submitting a review is one of the single best ways that you can help me keep *Power to Thrive* high in the search rank-ings. I am grateful in advance for your help with this.

You can mention Power to Thrive in blog post or through Facebook, LinkedIn, Twitter or upload a picture through Instagram.

Recommend Power to Thrive to those in your small group, book club, workplace, and classes.

Now go to the next page. Read through the *Power to Thrive* explanation of services. Take the coaching assessment and dis-cover your next step in living a *Power to Thrive* life. Everyone needs a coach in life, especially Christians!

Power to Thrive
Explanation of Services

I believe many people are stuck today and missing something in their life...

I believe that fear is rampant in our society today, paralyzing people from becoming everything that God created them to be...

I believe every Christian needs a coach to walk by their side and to help activate their power...

Why? I believe this because The Bible and anything Christian is continually demonized by the media, our education system, politics, and cultural divisions. The result of that is that people are moving away from the very source of power that can give them all they need.

So what I do is help people like you to rise above mediocrity, unlock your God-given power, and elevate your everyday living by activating your spirit drive.

What makes me different in the Christian coaching space is that I have a **unique coaching process** that links the Bible, Science, Psychology, and Personal Development together in a way that connects people to Jesus Christ like no other.

My unique process has helped people in many ways, including people who struggle in their marriages and relationships. People who have had no clue what their purpose is. And still others who had huge disconnects with the Lord God almighty. Others so encompassed with fear that they felt trapped in their everyday lives. But with every single one, they have found massive improvement in the quality of their lives, experienced profound change, and had a closer walk with the Lord. All by implementing the power to thrive process.

I have found that there are **three main groups of people** today who benefit from the Power to Thrive process:

1. People who are stuck or feel like something is missing in their life, whether they're Christian or not.

2. Those who are just not fed at their local church and who really hungry and thirsty for a closer walk with God and living as He created them to be.

3. Those who have a Christian background but are not living or embracing the Christian faith at this time but are feeling an inner voice calling them to get back to their roots. Seeking a deep and personal relationship with Jesus Christ again.

If I can help you do this as I have done for those people I just described, what would stop us from beginning a coaching relationship together?

Would Coaching Benefit You?

Everybody has a ceiling in their life—it's that point where you have gone as far as you can go with your insights, knowledge, and skill sets. If you are a person who wants to stop settling for mediocrity and break through your ceiling, now is the time to call in the experts. I believe that every Christian needs a coach in life. A coach can help you take your life to the next level of success, fulfillment, and happiness. The four core areas of your life are: Physical, Knowledge, Emotional, and Spiritual. Issues in these areas can lead to unfulfillment, unhappiness, and under-performance.

Please take just a few moments to find out how ready you are to live life to the fullest, be the best you can be, and explode through your ceiling with unlimited possibilities.

On a scale from 1 to 10, rate each of the following statements: (if not applicable, score the item a 5).

| 1 | 2 | 3 | 4 | 5 | 6 | 7 | 8 | 9 | 10 |

Don't agree at all   –   Somewhat agree   -Totally agree |

- I desire or need more balance in my life.

- I desire or need to improve my personal & or business relationships.

- I desire to make changes to my physical life.

- I desire or need to find and live my life's purpose.

- I am willing to overcome self-limiting beliefs and behavior.

- I desire or need to create plans and take action to achieve my goals.

- I desire or need more fulfillment at work and in my life.

- I desire or need to lessen the stress and anxiety I feel in my life.

- I desire to make more money and begin my financial freedom journey.

- I desire to have more energy and be happier with my life.

- I desire or need to have a closer walk with God and live for Him.

Add up your score.

Interpreting your score:

Under 30
Coaching is not for you right now.

31 to 60
Coaching could help you to look at your life from a different perspective, and help you create a plan to change what you would

like to change. However, you will need to make a decision, be committed, and take action in moving forward.

Over 60

Congratulations! You are ready for a relationship with a Coach! You are willing to do whatever it takes to create the life you deserve and desire.

Please take a moment right now and email Rich at Rich@ Richcavaness.com to help get you started living the life you were created to live. This one decision can change your life forever. If you prefer, you can go to Rich's website at www.RichCavaness. com to be contacted as well.

Next Steps to Living a Power to Thrive Life

Go to www.PowerToThrive.net to register for the Power to Thrive FREE Webinar Series from Rich.

Go to the Power to Thrive Facebook page and join the group to receive weekly FREE videos from Rich on Bible study, motivation, and personal development

Go to www.PowerToThrive.net to register for Rich's four weeks, 40-minute coaching series on the *#1 Bible Verse for Personal and Spiritual Success*

- Reserve Rich Cavaness for speaking engagements or team meetings

- ½ day or full-day training with workbook on The Power to Thrive concepts

Topics Include:

- The Gratitude Effect: How Mindset is the Key Denominator to Everything
- The Christian Playbook: 23 Principles of Personal Achievement
- The 13 Key Areas to Having a Thriving Relationship with Your Spouse
- The #1 Bible Verse for Personal and Spiritual Success

For Seminar or Coaching Information

Check out Rich's websites for FREE education, products, and seminar availability.

www.RichCavaness.com

Email: Rich@RichCavaness.com **or Phone: 214-924-5693**

Acknowledgments

I have to thank my wife Libia for putting up with me since November 2011 with my risk-taking mentality, entrepreneurship craziness, and burying myself in my computer for days on end writing and creating content. I also need to thank Libia for being patient with me in my spiritual walk over the years while I figured things out for myself. Love your Christian example to me and others; love your giving, serving, and desire for God. You inspire me to be the best man, husband, father, and grandfather I can be. Te Amo, my love.

Thank you to my Lord and Savior, Jesus Christ, for inspiring me and guiding me through the process of putting this book and its materials together. I am grateful that You created me with the gifts of teaching, evangelism, and exhortation. I love to help people improve their lives and become the best that You created them to be; thank You for putting that desire in my heart. Thank You, Jesus, for being patient with me. It's been a long and challenging journey to get back on track with my spiritual life. Every day the fire and passion for spending time with You come back stronger. I know the calling You have put on my life; I will step out by faith to accomplish it and walk in Your power, love, and with the Holy Spirit guiding my steps. I am a soul on fire for the calling placed on my life and the purpose placed in my heart.

To my daughter, Sarah and my son Jonathan, Mom and Dad, Sister, my entire family, and friends, thank you for allowing me to witness firsthand the power of love and forgiveness can have. I know I deeply hurt our family and relationship for a while, but each of you has shown me what it means to forgive and love your own family amid poor decisions, hurt, pain, lies, and distance. I love you so much for that, thank you.

To one of the best friends a person could have, Terry Loss, where would I be without your friendship? We have been through so much together since we first met in the early 90s. In my life, your support, advice, and patience blesses me. Thank you for always being there for me; your friendship has meant everything to me.

I have to thank The Road Leadership team for believing in me and giving me a second chance in leading, writing, creating, and making a difference in people's lives. The Road changed my life's entire direction and helped me to see the real me and understand the WHY's of my life. I will be forever grateful and blessed to be part of such a life-changing organization. www.TheRoadAdventure.org

To the guys at Cashflow Tactics, to say that you were a big part in allowing me to see and believe that I could put a plan in place and how to do that to be financially free in 10 years or less. Your teaching, mentoring, and support have been invaluable. I am grateful to all the thousands of people you give them hope, courage, and a system to make their dreams come true. www.CashflowTactics.com

And to all those hundreds of friends and teachers along the path of my life, too many to mention, whose insights, strategies, examples, love, and caring are the shoulders I have had the honor to stand on. I give thanks to you all, and I continue my never-ending quest to each day be a blessing in the lives of all those I have the privilege to meet, love, and serve.

About the Author

Rich Cavaness is an author, entrepreneur, certified master coach practitioner, speaker, former Senior Pastor, and sales and marketing specialist for several companies in Las Vegas and Dallas, TX.

Rich Cavaness has spoken to thousands of people in the field of Bible-based success and personal development, as well revivals and evangelism events for churches across the United States. Hundreds of people accepted Jesus Christ as their personal savior and also baptized through his powerful and simple teaching of the Gospel and God's word.

Rich has the unique and powerful ability to take any topic, especially Bible teachings, and make it easy for people to understand and apply to their lives. He teaches people today how to master the important areas of their lives: physically, mentally, emotionally, spiritually, financially, and in relationships.

For 8 years, Rich was an evangelist, revivalist, and Senior Pastor of churches in Charleston and Huntington, WV.

He has an extensive background in the insurance industry and has owned and operated two successful insurance agencies over 12-years. He currently operates Cavaness Insurance Agency out of Dallas, TX, a multi-line insurance agency specializing in life and property-casualty insurance. Farmers Insurance acknowledges him as a Top 10% agency in the country.

He is currently a Certified Master Coach Practitioner through the Certified Coaches Federation. His passion is helping people rise above mediocrity and be all that God created them to be.

Rich has authored five books, the Author Academy Awards nominated his 2018 release of *The Gratitude Effect* as one of the top 10 self-help books for that year. He was also one of the first Christian authors to respond in 2006 to The Secret, with his powerful book, *Decoding the Secret: The Law of Attraction from a Biblical Perspective.*

Rich's Top 5 Strengths are high achiever, strategist, learner, focus, and maximizer. These are very helpful when helping people reach their goals and dreams.

Rich enjoys anything in the mountains, visiting family, travel, exercise, and reading and research.

Rich has two adult children, two granddaughters, and he lives in Dallas, TX, with his wife, Libia.

"God has not given you the spirit of fear,
but of power, love, and sound mind."
2 Timothy 1:7

So many people in and out of the Christian faith feel stuck and that something is missing in their life, *Power to Thrive* **provides the GAME PLAN to help you rise above mediocrity.**

Power to Thrive means operating with your God-given gifts and talents so that you can wake up each day living with purpose and passion in your life.

Power to Thrive is about operating in strength and confidence vs. fear and timidity so that you can accomplish and live out everything God has created you to be and do.

Power to Thrive is about equipping yourself with the right mindset, understanding your true identity, and how to live your best life with your health, wealth, and relationships so that you can let your personal power out. God's desire for you is to **THRIVE!**

Power to Thrive is about learning that your thoughts, words, actions, habits, and values so that you can have more control over the outcomes of your life.

"Power to Thrive is not your typical self-help book. It is packed with scientific research and Biblical wisdom that will transform your life. Rich masterfully weaves anecdote and expertise to clearly show anyone how to Rise above mediocrity, Unlock your God-given power, and Elevate your everyday living." **David Jamieson, Senior Pastor of Church in the Valley, BC, Canada**

"Power to Thrive will get you thinking differently, bigger, and more focused on your true potential! Your real PURPOSE is right around the corner and starts on page 1 of this book. Very educational, inspiring

and motivating." **Cody Askins, #1 insurance sales trainer in the world**

Pick up a copy of *Power to Thrive* now so that you start living the life God created you for!

Rich Cavaness is a recognized speaker, author, and coach in the field of personal development and achievement and has the following credentials:

- 8 years of full-time ministry and was an ordained Senior Pastor for two churches

- Over the last 20 years has coached hundreds of people on Bible-based success principles

- Certified Master Coach Practitioner with the Certified Coaches Federation

- Entrepreneur and Acquisition Entrepreneur and Insurance industry expert